TOTAL HOME PROTECTION

A Successful Book

TOTAL HOME PROTECTION
A Successful Book

Curt Miller

STRUCTURES PUBLISHING COMPANY
Farmington, Michigan   1976

Manufactured in the United States of America

Book edited by Shirley M. Horowitz
Book designed by Richard Kinney
Current Printing (last digit)
10 9 8 7 6 5 4 3 2 1

International Standard Book Number: 0-912336-22-6 (hardcover)
0-912336-23-4 (softcover)

Library of Congress Catalog Card Number: 75-38407

Structures Publishing Co.

Library of Congress Cataloging in Publication Data

Miller, Curt.
     Total home protection.

     (A Successful book)
     Includes index.
     1. Burglary protection. 2. Dwellings—Fires
and fire prevention. 3. Home accidents—Prevention.
I. Title.
TH9745.D85M54   643   75-38407
ISBN 0-912336-22-6
ISBN 0-912336-23-4 pbk.

contents

introduction

One in every five homes will be burglarized this year; in the supposed safety of the average American neighborhood, a burglary will be committed at least once every 12 seconds. More than 700,000 fires strike American homes each year—at least one every minute. Seven thousand or more deaths result from these fires each year. In addition, home accidents account for thousands of deaths or debilitating injuries yearly. It appears inevitable, then, that your home will be the scene of a burglary, a fire, or a serious accident within the next few years.

The burglar will hit you for anywhere from forty cents to many thousands of dollars. If he encounters a member of your family while going about his work, he may be driven to violence. Accidents in the home total billions of dollars in annual losses attributable to lost work time, insurance administration costs, and medical costs. Even the termites beneath your feet eat up your dollars, by literally chewing the floors out from under you.

This all sounds a bit alarmist, doesn't it? But statistics show that the odds are against your escaping all of these threats, because burglary, fire, and accidents are increasing at an alarming rate. What does this mean to the homeowner? You will pay the costs in the form of increased insurance premiums, in loss of property, in loss of sleep, and perhaps in the loss of one you love. You will pay when the mailman trips on one of your children's skates, or when a lightning bolt hits your home, or when a small fire causes extensive smoke damage.

Many enforcement agencies blame owners for the increases in fires and burglaries. Carelessness has become the biggest stumbling block to reduction of burglaries, and a major reason for high accident rates, property loss due to fire, and personal injury from electric shock, and poisoning.

Your job is to reduce the desirability of your home as a burglary target by making it hard for the thief to enter, and escape, without detection; to eliminate the hazards that will cause human or property loss from fire; and to cover yourself for other external threats to your safety and property.

This book will show you how to prevent fires and how to prevent accidents by using commonsense and by teaching your children the dangers of carelessness. It will recommend the equipment you need to fight fires and the best means to escape injury once a fire occurs. Finally, it will teach you how to think like a thief so you can learn how to outwit the burglar. You will see:

- pictures and descriptions of how burglars work;

- how to install your own locks;
- how to protect doors and windows;
- how to install simple or complex alarm systems;
- how to prevent fires and how to react to them;
- specific products designed to detect, warn of, and put out fires;
- the major causes of accidents and how to reduce the probability of an accident on your property;
- that many low-cost and commonsense measures are available to you at little or no cost.

If you are just planning or building a new house or are deciding where to move, you will be able to avoid costly mistakes and know which types of neighborhoods to avoid. And to help you find out which information you need and where to get it, we suggest that you take the security audit at the end of the book and consult the manufacturers list provided.

Whatever you do, do not wait until after a fire, a burglary, or a serious accident to implement your home protection plan. The time to get started is now.

section 1 Home Security

we are all victims

There is one chance in five that the place you call home will be burglarized this year. It seems inevitable, then, that you will be robbed in the next five years.

By any measurement crime is an ominous problem. Since 1961 rates for all serious crimes have more than doubled. In just a one year period—from 1973 to 1974—serious crime jumped 17 percent (the largest increase since uniform national statistics have been available). The future is not hopeless, however. This book will show you what you are up against and how to combat the burglar while protecting yourself, your property, and your family.

What does this mean to the homeowner? In 1966 burglaries cost American homeowners $284 million. In 1972, approximately 2,300,000 burglaries cost the public $465 million. In 1973, according to the FBI Uniform Crime Report, burglaries increased 20 percent. The 2,540,900 burglaries committed that year cost property owners nearly $5.5 million. This does not include the actual damage that may be done to a home when it is burglarized—broken windows or doors, or senseless vandalism. Although the cost of stolen goods amounts to only about $225 per burglary, this represents an average; there is no telling on which side of the statistical balance you will be. Too, it represents only the tip of the proverbial iceberg.

It is estimated that actual burglaries may total three times the reported burglaries. Many burglaries go unreported either because a relative is involved, or because the victim fears reprisals from the burglar or from the police. Living in a suburban area does nothing to protect you from the burglar. Although cities still have the highest rate of crime, the suburbs have a higher rate of increase—up 20 percent last year. In fact it now seems that burglars are becoming reverse commuters, heading toward the suburbs to carry on their work, while suburbanites are in the city pursuing their careers. In the last five years daytime burglaries of residences have gone up 56 percent.

Statistics, though, don't come alive until you, a relative or a close friend, are added to the nation's statistical profile of crime. And your chances of coming out of a burglary unscathed—with nothing more than a property loss—are growing dim. For although the "professional" burglar will take every precaution to enter your home only while you are away, more and more young, inexperienced burglars are becoming involved. It is hard to draw a profile of the criminal, but one fact is clear: teenagers and young adults made up half the number of those arrested last year. And 15 is the peak age for perpetrators of violent crime. You'll find many 15 year olds among the growing number

of white middle-class gangs operating in the suburbs, burglarizing and terrorizing their victims. They
are generally in a hurry, and care little whether
or not they run into you when they are burglarizing
your home. They snub their noses at you and at
law enforcement authorities, figuring that if they
run into you while ransacking your house in search
of cash or stereo components, their sheer numbers
will frighten you off.

One gang of youths, living in a well-to-do suburb
of Buffalo, New York, was responsible for dozens
of thefts, including bicycles, lawn mowers, and
television sets. The gang members were often
observed in acts of burglary by homeowners who
quickly telephoned the police. Yet they were always
out of sight by the time the police arrived. The
gangleader carried a radio which monitored police
calls, and if a unit were being dispatched to the
scene of their operations, he knew about it.

Another young and often violent burglar is the
addict. Urgently in need of a fix, he will not take
the time to case your house in order to find out
if anyone is home. If it appears unoccupied to him
at first glance, or if he happens to stumble upon
an open door, he will walk right in.

If luck is on your side he will make off with your
property and leave. But if you, your spouse or
children are home, you may frighten him. And like
a trapped animal who reacts violently, he will attack
you. If you think this information about addicts
is included to dramatize our point, you're wrong.
Maybe dead wrong. In New York City, way back
in the good old days—1969—it was reported that
New York's heroin users might be stealing as much
as $2.6 billion a year in property to support their
habits. But that is the big city, perhaps you don't
live in a big city—what do you have to worry about?

Plenty. No matter where he lives, the addict must
steal constantly. When he fences (sells) his stolen
goods, he may receive as little as 10 percent of
their value. And the number of heroin addicts has
multiplied 12 times in the last 10 years, according to the Justice Department's Office of National Narcotics Intelligence. There are now at least
600,000 addicts in this country. Obviously they do
not all live in New York. They are scattered
throughout the nation. Take Albuquerque, for example. In 1969, 75 percent of the burglaries in that
city were reportedly committed by addicts.

To say the least, the outlook is depressing. Pre-
liminary reports to the FBI in 1975 indicate that
this year's increase in crime will probably be worse
than ever. One obvious reason is unemployment.
Although white collar jobs may be difficult to find,
you need little experience to become a burglar.
And because of lax laws and an overworked legal
system, the potential rewards of crime far outweigh
the potential punishment.

To complicate matters, says urban designer
Oscar Newman, the small-town and neighborhood
environments that once kept crime in check are
breaking down or disappearing. We have become
a nation of strangers. In most cities people are
only barely acquainted with one another and have
only minimal contact with their next door neighbors. They share common beliefs about few things,
and while a majority may agree that crime must
be stopped, they offer a general-store variety of
solutions.

Consequently, there is little chance that a community will band together to solve its own crime
problems (there are a few notable exceptions which
will be discussed later). And without unified community support for police action, according to
Newman, in many neighborhoods the police can
inflame rather than cure the crime problem.

It is no wonder, then, that police cannot seem to stem the increasing tide of criminality. They cite shortage of manpower and money as the main reasons, along with a growing mistrust of the police. Augmenting the police are many private security agencies that can provide some degree of protection to the homeowner. However they suffer even greater financial limitations than the police department. Also, the desire by a small number of private agencies to turn a fast buck has led to numerous instances of hiring of unqualified personnel, and scattered instances of the hiring of criminals. These failures by policing agencies leave the burden of protection on you, the home-owner.

But in general, the homeowner has done little to stop burglary. In fact some law enforcement agencies blame homeowners for its increase, citing carelessness as the cause (9 out of 10 times a burglar can find an open door or window through which he can enter your house). This carelessness is indeed the biggest stumbling block to cutting down on burglary.

We hear dozens of people who say they never have to lock their doors because "no one around here would rob us." These are the same people who act indignant after being robbed, and blame the police. Then there are those who refuse to take security precautions because they think any crook who wants to get into their house will, "so why bother with the expense?"

To a certain extent they are right: Any professional burglar who has the incentive (in terms of a possible lucrative haul from your home) and is well prepared, will be able to enter your home. He will have the proper tools and burglary technology, will try to find a period when there is plenty of time for him to accomplish his task, and will succeed in his business by really trying.

Most burglars, however, are not so professional. Like the casual shoplifter, we find many a casual burglar. They are looking for the easy mark. They would rather walk into your home through an unlocked door or window than take the time to break in and risk discovery. Your job is to reduce the desirability of your house as a burglary target.

We will show you how to think like a thief so you will learn what the burglar looks for, and how he operates when he burglarizes your home.

Take a walk down your own block. Do you think the burglar would try to steal from your house, with its well-lit grounds, five-foot picket fence, and growling Doberman? Or would he rather visit Nelson, your neighbor, who has one small porch light, no fence, and a lot of overhanging trees, providing a protected view from the street?

We think the answer is obvious.

In this book you will:

—See pictures of and read descriptions of burglars in operation;
—Learn how to install your own locks;
—Learn how to protect doors and windows;
—Learn how to install alarm systems, from simple magnetic switches to microwaves and ultrasonics;
—Discover that there are many commonsense security measures available to you at little or no cost. Trimming that six-foot hedge in front of your house, for example, could reduce your vulnerability 50 percent.

If you are just beginning to plan a new house or are deciding where to move, this book will enable you to avoid costly mistakes. And whether you are moving or staying put, we advise you to take the security audit at the end of this book to beef up your security.

"burglarproof" doors and windows

There is no such thing as a burglarproof home. Or at least there wasn't until we came along. Available technology, some of it ultra modern and some ancient, has made it possible for us to invent the Ultra-Perfect Secret Security System. Here's how it works.

Your house is surrounded by a six-foot-high chain link fence with 50,000 volts of electricity surging through it. If a burglar touches the fence the current begins to surge through him. If he attempts to cut the fence with insulated wire cutters, an alarm sounds. If somehow he gets over the fence, a passive infrared detector senses his body heat, triggering an automatic dialer which phones the nearest police station and delivers a prerecorded message alerting the police to the intrusion on your property. At the same time the kennel doors spring open, letting loose the dozen or so Dobermans your gate keeper cares for.

If the burglar manages to elude the hounds, perhaps with a ready supply of bones other than his own, he is confronted with a heavy-gauge steel door with a pickproof lock. In a matter of minutes he manages to blow the door open with explosives and is standing inside your front vestibule.

Unfortunately the burglar did not realize that unauthorized opening of the door activates the laser beam, which cuts him to pieces.

It sounds like a scene from a James Bond fantasy. But the technology is available. If you wish, you can protect your home in this manner, at great expense. The determined burglar, however, could probably still enter your home.

Let's repeat our statement from the beginning of this chapter with a correction:

THERE IS NO SUCH THING AS A
BURGLARPROOF HOME AND THERE NEVER
WILL BE!

In burglar alarm technology the goal is to try to stay a few years ahead of the common criminal. But law enforcement officials recognize that anything one man can invent another man can defeat, whether it is a simple lock or a sophisticated alarm system. This book is not intended to spread paranoia. Rather, it will show you that with common sense and whatever your budget may allow, whether it be $5 or $5,000, you can beef up your home's security and make it unlikely that a burglar will strike.

BASIC DEFENSES

Your job is to make your home as unattractive as possible to the potential burglar. This does not mean that you forget to paint it. It does mean that you must keep your home in good repair and give it a warm, lived-in, cared-for look. Burglary is a crime of opportunity. If the burglar does not see evidence of carelessness at first glance he will move on.

Doors and windows are your first line of defense. These convenience devices allow you to enter and leave your home, but at the same time make a burglar's job much easier.

Doors

Your family makes use of house doors many times a day. So it is no wonder that the burglar considers this method of entering the home first. In fact, in a study done in the area around Washington, D.C., it was found that in more than 63 percent of all residential burglaries, the thieves entered through a door. And unfortunately, in too many cases the reason for the easy entry was a door left open by a careless homeowner.

Even if you do remember to lock your door it remains vulnerable. While there are many good lock pickers on the street who can open your door without a key as easily as you can with a key, they are not your major worry as long as you have a fairly good pick-resistant lock cylinder. Too often, we have seen $100 pushbutton or other high-security locks installed on doors which can be easily forced and offer only ten cents worth of protection. Of course, any locked door is a psychological deterrent, but you need more than that. Despite the fact that advertisements and pitches from salesmen emphasize the importance of a lock, a lock is only as good as the door on which it is installed. Doors which are chosen for their attractiveness rather than their soundness, can be easily broken through by the burglar who uses brute force to enter your home.

Several aspects of door construction which make the burglar's job easier include:

(1) outside hinges;
(2) rotting door or frame;
(3) too much space between door and frame;
(4) poorly constructed door—too thin or with wood or glass panels;

(5) poor construction of entire frame and door buck area.

Using this list as a guide, you should consider checking and repairing your doors the first task in your home protection plan.

Check the side and back doors of your house. For some reason homeowners neglect the security of these doors, considering them to be less important than the front door, which must be kept up for appearances' sake. Often you will find the back door has undergone a rotting process; a settling-in process often comes along with this. While the door and frame may have fit snugly when the house was first built, there may be a gap between door and frame by now. So, first check for door fit. Examine the space between the door and the frame. While an opening of about 1/16th of an inch looks fine to you, it looks even better to the burglar. With a space that large he can insert a screwdriver or crowbar and force or "jimmy" the lock so that it pulls away from the frame, and the bolt or latch portion pops out of the receiver in the door frame. Or, if the bolt does not pop out of place, he can create a space large enough to insert a hacksaw and then saw through the bolt.

To prevent this, you should try to keep the space between door and door frame down to 1/64th of an inch.

There are several ways to accomplish this. The method most difficult, and at the same time the most permanent, is to drive a few wedges of wood between the door frame and the door buck (which is actually a frame for the frame). This will help close the gap from inside the wall. Or you can take the door off its hinges and secure a strip of wood or steel from top to bottom, in effect widening the door. You can do this on hinge or lock side of the door, but the hinge side tends to be more secure.

Other possibilities include driving some closely spaced nails through the frame about six inches above and below the lock. This helps lessen the clearance in the area of the lock, making it more difficult for the burglar to force the latch from its receiver.

If the frame is rotting, the crook can first use

his crowbar as a chisel to remove some of the wood, widening his working space, creating the same problems as above. Looking to the other side of the door, the burglar can also use a crowbar to pull the door open on the hinge side. Since doors with outside hinges are usually found on older homes, it is highly likely that the frame is rotting, or the metal on the hinge plate is rusted. Inserting a crowbar, the crook can easily rip the hinges out of a rotting frame, or off a rotting door.

To prevent this from occurring, examine the screws. They may be too short. Or there may be only two screws holding a hinge plate intended to be secured with four. Before you replace them, examine the wood beneath the screws to determine if it should be replaced. Replacing half inch screws with one inch screws wll do little good if the wood has rotted through. If you doubt the strength of the wood, buy wooden blocks to be used on the inside of the door as supports for the weak wood. Buy screws which are long enough to go through both the hinge plate and the door and which embed deeply into the wooden blocks. Make sure the screws are nonretractable. Special screws are available which can be screwed into your door but not removed. Other screws available can be inserted or removed only with a special device.

All of the above suggestions are to be used if you do not plan to completely replace your outside-hinged door. Personally, I recommend against doors with hinge pins on the outside. A New York City police captain told us that once the hinge pins are removed a lock will often serve as an excellent swinging device for the burglar to use when opening the door. If you must keep your present hinged door there are hinge pins available which are said to be nonremovable. Ask about them at large hardware stores or home improvement centers.

Door frames

If the door frame is so poor that none of these measures will help it, remove it. A chisel should do the trick. Replace the frame with good, strong wood and make sure you attach it securely to the door framing or masonry. You should be able to do this yourself if you are at all handy. But if large home improvement projects are not your specialty, hire a carpenter and make sure he knows it is proper fit, not speed, that you are looking for.

Another feature of door frame construction that often attracts the burglar is its unsturdiness. For security purposes the door frame can be made of wood or metal, but it had better be good. While the frame in the old home may be rotting, reducing the effectiveness of the door, the frame in a new home may be only a little better. Modern construction techniques often incorporate haste into homebuilding. To avoid snags at the time of construction, door bucks are built which are purposely oversize. This ensures that the frame will fit easily into the buck. The frame is then secured by thin wooden wedges inserted at two or three points on either side of the door. The area is then plastered over.

But how secure is it? Often a gap of one inch is compensated for with multiple layers of thin wooden wedges. Time and repeated slamming of the door may jar some of the wedges loose and the frame may be hanging in up to an inch of air space. Whenever confronted with the unsturdy frame the burglar can use a crowbar with no problem. If he is a professional and has the time and the inclination, he may use a method of breaking and entering that baffles both you and your insurance company. If the thief comes equipped with an auto jack he can stretch the frame just above the lock. The flexible frame stretches as the jack expands. Eventually the frame is spread wide enough for the bolt to be pulled out of its place in the lock strike. The thief opens the door, takes what he came for and leaves without a trace. Chances are the frame will return to its original position and there will be no signs of forcible entry. You will be unable to prove to your insurance company that your house was broken into, and you may have trouble collecting on your homeowner's policy.

If you cannot replace the frame you might try a jimmy guard. Simply, it is an angle iron with an L-shaped section that is mounted on the frame, opposite the lock. It acts as a protective covering, protecting the deadbolt from attack if the frame is spread apart. When you mount the jimmy guard, be sure to use nonretractable screws.

Reinforcing your door

If your door is a thing of beauty to you, with its series of wooden or glass panels or with that extravagant opaque window, it is also a thing of beauty to the burglar. There is not a burglar around who cannot hammer, kick, or even punch his way through the thin wooden panels of your door. And glass presents even less of a problem. Once a panel or window is broken, the burglar reaches inside to unlock the door.

To protect yourself from this type of attack you need a flush hardwood door without any panels or windows. If your door does have panels, you have two choices:

(1) replace the door,
(2) reinforce the door.

If you opt to replace the door you should have little trouble. Take accurate measurements and head to your home improvement center. You need a door that is 1-3/4 to 2 inches thick, made of hardwood or metal with a solid core. Before installing a new door make sure the existing hinges can take the weight of your new, heavier door. If in doubt, buy heavier hinges and longer screws.

To reinforce the door, some security writers recommend taking the door off its hinges, filling the panels with concrete, then covering the door with plywood to resemble a flush door. We think that unless you are a pro at concrete work, replacing the door is a more viable solution. But you can accomplish almost the same thing by securing a 3/4 inch panel of plywood or a piece of sheet metal, measured to size, to your door. This can usually be done while the door is on its hinges. Installing the panel on the outside of the door serves as both a physical and a psychological deterrent because the exposed panels are covered over.

Another important addition to your home protection can be a door closer. Often a thief will follow a woman who is struggling with a large bundle. Usually she will open the door, hurry into the kitchen to drop her bundle, and then return to close the door. A burglar following close behind can sneak into the house and remain in hiding until he sees his chance to burglarize the house, or he can just attack the woman. Either way it is much safer to have a hydraulic or spring-operated door closer which quickly forces the door closed. You should examine your family's habits to decide if such a device is necessary, and on which door(s) these devices should be installed.

Following the methods above your door will be safe from most burglary attacks. But some burglars have another method of housebreaking. They use a sabre saw to cut around the lock and then open the door, leaving the lock hanging in air. This is easy to take care of on a wooden door: drill quarter inch holes several inches above and below the lock, and insert long metal pins or threaded rods which are slightly smaller in both diameter and length than the holes you have cut into the door. Then seal the holes with wood putty and finish them. In effect your door is now reinforced in a manner similar to that used in bank vaults.

If you are renting a home and the landlord has written a provision into your lease that prevents you from replacing or reinforcing the door, you should install a double cylinder lock which requires a key to open it from both the inside and the outside. If a burglar breaks through a panel and reaches inside he will be confronted with a lock rather than a knob. And burglars who use force are generally not sophisticated enough to also pick locks. Therefore you are reasonably safe, unless the burglar becomes so frustrated that he uses a sledgehammer to break all of the panels and crawl through the door. For fire safety reasons, never lock the double cylinder lock while you are at home.

If you live in a home with a vestibule or closed-in porch that leads to the front door, secure it with a lock. Otherwise the burglar can enter the vestibule and have cover in which to work.

Sliding doors

Sliding glass doors, the kind that usually face onto your patio, almost always come with a flimsy lock. Richard S. Clark of Adams Rite Manufacturing Co., which makes locks for glass doors, says the problem with these doors is that "many people don't even consider them doors. They call them sliding glass walls."

Indeed, these doors do appear to be walls. And nobody ever worries about the security of their

Windows are prime targets for daytime burglars, who find it easy to force them open with simple tools.

The Protect-A-Guard window gate from Windor Security Systems makes it nearly impossible for a burglar to break into your house through the window, but provides easy egress for your family. Inset shows that even a child can operate the locking knob, which is protected from outside attack by steel box casing.

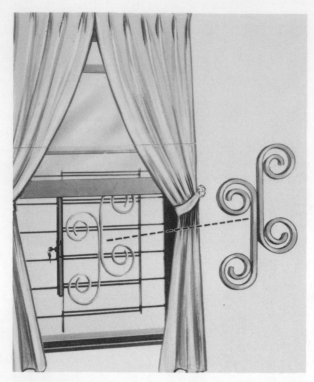

Heavy-duty metalwork keeps burglars and burglary tools away from vulnerable windows (Windor photo).

walls. But because they provide a large access area, says Clark, they must be secured by a "real lock, a secure lock and a lock that can be operated with a key" (all, of course, the same lock).

The problem with sliding doors, and the reason few manufacturers supply locks for them, is that they have very narrow stiles and are vulnerable to being jimmied. And in the door there is usually very little room to mount the traditional horizontal throw bolt or latch. Adams Rite has a special lock with a pivoted latch which, when not in use, lies vertically in the housing, making it possible to have a long throw bolt in a limited space. Loxem also has a good, inexpensive lock for sliding doors. It is lightweight and comes in a kit for easy homeowner installation. The lock has a cylinder-operated deadbolt and tamperproof screws as extra security features. Sliding doors can also be protected by alarm foil or magnetic switches wired to an alarm circuit.

All nonglass doors should be equipped with a method for viewing or interviewing visitors without opening the door. A wide angle viewer inserted in a small hole drilled at eye level in the door

Attractive metalwork designs are available to keep burglars from entering your house through vulnerable windows while at the same time serving as a decoration for your home.

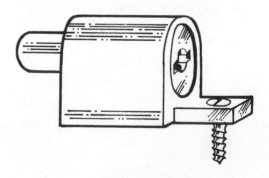

The Yale Window Lock is used on double-hung windows to secure them in the closed or ventilation position. The bolt slips into a hole drilled into the upper window frame.

is a big help. To receive letters or packages you should consider installing a heavy-duty chain which allows you to open the door part way without exposing yourself to an attack.

Windows

Unless you live in a Spanish-style house with its many windows facing onto a large courtyard, your house probably has a dozen or more externally exposed windows, and a dozen or more weak spots. We are not telling you to cut down on the number of windows planned for your new house. Certainly no one would cut down on windows for security reasons alone. And unless you are both ecology- and economy-minded you will not believe that the amount of heat you lose through these thin panels of glass causes soaring gas and electric bills.

Instead we will show you how to protect these vulnerable strips of glass which allow you to see out of the house, and allow the burglar to get in.

Usually windows have some kind of locking device. Put this book down and check each of your windows to make sure they are locked. Unless each window is locked you might as well send out engraved invitations inviting burglars to come to your home, because when a burglar enters a house through the window, nine out of ten times he does not have to break in. He almost always finds an open window.

Let's make the job of window protection both easy and economical. Not every window needs the same degree of protection, with its associated costs. Some windows are more accessible than others, and those are the windows on which to spend the most time and money. Windows which can be reached, but not as easily, should be given secondary consideration.

Briefly, any windows which are at ground floor level or face onto a porch or fire escape, are easily accessible and must be well secured. Second-story windows take more effort for the burglar to reach. He must come equipped with a ladder, or at least a rope, to lower himself from your roof, before he can enter the home through an unsecured second-story window. For this reason the "reachable" windows do not need the same degree of protection as the accessible windows.

To protect your windows you need one or more of the following devices:

 (1) a window lock;
 (2) small decorative panes;
 (3) a window gate;
 (4) burglar-resistant glass; or
 (5) protective, decorative metalwork.

Window locks

There are dozens of gadgets on the market which will hold your windows closed without actually locking them. They range from the standard sash lock which comes on nearly all double-hung windows, to a rubber wedge device which is screw-tightened to hold the windows in place.

The sash lock is not really a lock at all. It is a latch, consisting of a curved metal arm and a receptacle. The two pieces, in practice, are supposed to mesh, drawing the windows tightly together. However, poor construction techniques, poor mounting of the device, or warping of the window due to age, can render the device useless. Think about the number of sash locks in your home which fit poorly or do not work at all, perhaps because they have been painted over so many times.

If the burglar cannot find a sash lock that does not work, he will look for windows that fit poorly. Sometimes the fit is so poor he can simply jiggle the windows to open the sash lock. Or, if he chooses to smash or cut your window, he simply has to reach inside and open the lock.

The wedge lock with a rubber tip mounts on the upper frame portion of the lower window. Turning it exerts pressure on the upper window frame, supposedly holding it shut and locked. Its principle is self-defeating. It holds the windows shut by spreading them apart. This makes it easy for a burglar to slip a knife blade between the windows and cut off the rubber piece. In addition, years of use often wear down the rubber, making it easy for the crook to exert a little extra effort to lift your window. Again, if he chooses to cut your window he can reach inside and loosen the device.

What you really need for window protection is a window lock with a key. Even if the burglar breaks your window he must contend with a lock. If you use a high-quality lock, available for only a few dollars, you have made his job more difficult.

Protect all windows in your house with window locks and have all locks keyed alike. Give each family member a key and keep one or two keys near the window, within easy reach of children, but away from the groping hands of a burglar. Why two keys? In case of fire, with its associated panic, it is possible to drop one key. A second key should be immediately available.

Window locks are usually installed with self-tapping screws on the lower window frame. A hole is drilled into the upper frame into which the bolt slips. A second hole may be drilled a few inches higher so the window may be secured while in a ventilation position. A rule of thumb, though, is to never leave the window open more than five or six inches for ventilation purposes. Burglary tools or lean arms can be slipped through an opening any larger than that.

Paneled windows

Instead of a single window pane 30 by 40 inches, why not have your architect design windows incorporating many smaller panes, either square or diamond-shaped? Whether they are joined with wood or metal makes little difference because either way they make a window smasher's job more difficult. If your window has a lock on it, the burglar would have to smash each of the panes to crawl through the window. Experience has shown this to be unlikely because burglars do not like the resulting excessively loud noises, which tend to advertise their activities.

Window gates

Especially important to the apartment dweller, window gates can also be effectively used by the homeowner and indeed are recommended in high crime areas. The gates are basically an accordian-like arrangement of strong metal bars and cross members. They slide within a steel channel which is anchored by screws at both the top and bottom of the window frame. Many of the window gates rely on padlocks to keep them shut and to keep out burglars. However, because they present a

potential safety hazard in case of fire, they have been outlawed in many cities.

One company that supplies window gates without padlocks is Windor Security Systems, which manufactures the Protect-A-Gard window gate. Instead of using a padlock, the Windor gate uses a knob which is in turn protected within a small metal box attached to the gate. It is easy for you or even your children to open the gate, but because of the small distance between the gate's members if is impossible for a burglar to reach the knob.

You can install this gate yourself, or have a locksmith do it for you. You may find window gates in your home improvement center or large hardware store, or you may have to order one from the manufacturer. Be sure to measure the window's height precisely. If the window frame is rotting slightly or is otherwise weak, you should secure the gate to the masonry below it. Head to a hardware store and buy bolts several inches long. Using a masonry bit on your drill, you will have no trouble making a truly secure installation.

Decorative metalwork

Many companies supply grillwork that will prevent the burglar from entering your home through the window, while serving as a decoration at the same time. It's a neat trick and one we recommend.

When mounting metalwork make sure to place it far enough from the window to make it difficult for the burglar to reach the glass with his cutting tool. Make sure you buy a heavy-duty product and mount it securely with nonretractable screws.

You might want to grow some ivy around the metalwork, if it is in keeping with the overall theme of your house. An added benefit of the metal work is that it can keep small children from trying to fly out of second story windows.

Burglar-resistant glass

If you have ever had a baseball come flying through your window you know that while breaking a window is noisy, it is quite easy. Fortunately most burglars do not like to make noise and most often will attempt not to break a window. However if your neighborhood is exceptionally noisy, a burglar can camouflage his activities with neighborhood noises like the cheering during a baseball game, or the sound of a passing truck.

In order to prevent this type of entry you might want to buy high-security windows originally inteded for banks and jewelry stores, made of glazed glass or special plastic. Amerada Glass Company supplies a laminated glass which resists repeated forceful attacks. The secret is that it has three panes, the middle one made of tough vinyl. After repeated blows with a sledgehammer the outside panes will shatter, but the vinyl will be unscathed.

Lexan, available from General Electric, is a high-strength plastic which can be used for residential security purposes. Unlike other plastics, Lexan is highly mar-resistant. Both types of special-purpose glass run from about two to five times the price of ordinary window glass, but if you have a large picture window that worries you, security glass is probably a more logical choice than metalwork or a window gate.

Quick window security

Windows you never use, such as basement windows, should be nailed shut. If some basement windows must be left open for ventilation, make a mental note to check them each time you leave the house, because they are the windows most often left open.

To close windows you don't want to spend much money securing, you can use metal pins. On double-hung windows a hole is drilled into both the upper and lower portions of the window frame. A metal pin, slightly smaller than the hole, is inserted into the hole. It will be invisible from the outside and serves the same purpose as nailing a window shut. However the window can be opened by using a magnet to withdraw the pin from the hole. You can also drill added holes to secure the window into a position for ventilation.

For casement windows you can use a similar method by drilling a hole entirely through the latching device. Make sure it is nearly as wide as the hole and no longer than the hole. To disengage the pin, push it out with a screwdriver, nail or pen.

Protection can be added to any type of window using alarm foil and magnetic switches connected to an alarm system. Examine your budget, though, before you decide that an alarm system is essential. The purpose of this book is to show you how to spend as little as possible to protect your home most effectively.

locks and entry devices

The variety of locks and locking technologies available to keep a burglar out of your house is staggering. But before looking at the more basic of these locking devices, let's look at some of the ways a burglar can circumvent them. This will help you make a sensible decision about which locks you need for your house.

Basically there are seven classifications of burglars who assault your locks in an attempt to enter your home. they are:

(1) celluloid or "loid"user;
(2) pickman;
(3) drillman;
(4) cylinder puller;
(5) set screw loosener;
(6) lock forcer; and
(7) keyman.

As you can see, the names of these criminals more or less describe how they operate.

The celluloid, or loid user, relies on a credit card or other thin piece of plastic to enter your home. If you have a lock that latches automatically when you slam the door, you will be this man's target. The latch which holds your door in place is tapered. By inserting a credit card between the door and frame, the thief can push back the latch and open your door.

The lockman, or pickman, uses either a few pieces of bent metal, some illegally purchased or self-fashioned lock picks, or even a lock-picking gun. The picks are designed to manipulate the pins inside the tumbler of the lock until they all line up at a point called the shear line, at which point the cylinder can be turned with a small tension wrench, and the door can be opened. This is the same principle on which a key operates, so it is understandable that, using the same method, the pickman will be quite successful. If he is more sophisticated, the pickman will have a pick gun, which makes a series of loud noises as its probe end jangles the pins into place. Most locks can be picked in 30 seconds or less by the experienced pickman. Fortunately there are many high-quality cylinders available which operate on different principles than the standard cylinder, and come close to being pickproof.

The drillman is less skilled than the pickman but may know the same principles. He may drill a very small hole above the keyway and insert a device which can hold the cylinder pins in place. Or, more likely, he will drill out the keyway—attack it with a drill until the pin system is rendered useless and the door can be opened simply by turning the doorknob.

The number of cylinder pullers seems to be

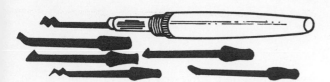

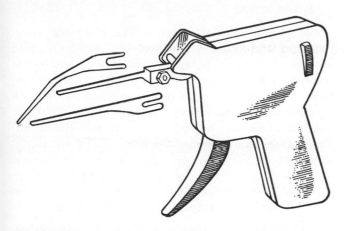

A lock pick set (available only to locksmiths) is designed to resemble a fountain pen. Six different probes are shown, but most locksmiths say they can pick a lock with one or two probes, at most.

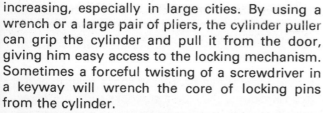

The pick gun, used by locksmith and burglar alike, vibrates pins into position within the cylinder. A tension wrench is then used to turn the tumbler core.

Fichet's Vertibar, high-security locking system is said to resist all physical attacks and attempts at picking. Note recesses in door frame and on ceiling—each is a locking point. There are five deadbolts and two dog bolts. A ten-lever cylinder incorporated in the Vertibar is virtually pickproof.

increasing, especially in large cities. By using a wrench or a large pair of pliers, the cylinder puller can grip the cylinder and pull it from the door, giving him easy access to the locking mechanism. Sometimes a forceful twisting of a screwdriver in a keyway will wrench the core of locking pins from the cylinder.

The set screw loosener can practice his trade only on mortise locks, those that are installed inside the door and by its edge. He poses as a charity solicitor and when you ask him to stand by the door while you go inside to get him money he unscrews one of the screws on the faceplate of the lock. This screw holds the cylinder in place. At night the burglar will return and simply remove the cylinder with a lightweight pair of pliers and then deactivate the locking mechanism.

The lock forcer comes equipped with a crowbar or large screwdriver to jimmy your door. By inserting a crowbar between the door and the frame he can force the bolt to pop from its place in the door. If you use one of the better locks, the lock forcer actually becomes a door breaker because it is the door and not the lock that eventually gives.

The keyman has either stolen a key which you thought you had misplaced, or bought a masterkey from someone in your apartment building, or copied the code number on your key and had a new key made in a key duplicating shop. Careless people make his job too easy. We will give you some ideas on how to keep your keys safe later in this section.

TYPES OF LOCKS AVAILABLE

Burglars are not interested in challenges. They do not like to take time trying to pick or force three locks when they can go down the block and find a neighbor with only one lock. While even the best locks cannot stop the determined burglar, they can slow him down, and this is what you are counting on.

There are three common types of locks used to keep your door shut. Some do nothing more than latch the door so a gust of wind will not blow

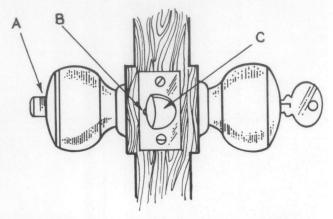

Key-in-knob lock. This is the easiest lock to install. Locking button (A), is located inside house. Trigger bolt (B), is depressed when the door closes, preventing latch (C), from being opened with a piece of celluloid.

Before your builder selects locking hardware you should talk to him about using decorative locks. The Schlage Stonehedge, pictured here, will fit into many decors.

it open, others help slow down the burglar—some, enough to discourage the burglar from breaking into your home. They include:

(1) key-in-knob locks;
(2) mortise locks; and
(3) rim locks.

Key-in-knob locks: These range from the very insecure, flimsy type, to those that are well constructed and fairly safe. You will find these locks in many tract homes or in any other home where the builder wanted to cut down on costs by making installation easier. Using a template supplied by the manufacturer, two holes are cut into the door. The advantage is that key-in-knob locks are fairly standard in size. If you have an old or flimsy key-in-knob lock, you can probably replace it with a newer, better model with little work.

There are several disadvantages, however:

(1) The locking mechanism is in the knob, outside the house. A strong man with a sledgehammer can easily break some of the cheaper versions of this type of lock.
(2) These locks use a tapered latch to hold the door shut. This type of latch can be defeated in a matter of seconds by the loid user.
(3) The latches are usually quite short and prone to jimmying.

To overcome these problems some manufacturers have introduced key-in-knob locks with added features. A trigger bolt, for example, is a semi-circular bolt attached to the latch in such a way that it prevents the latch from being slid out of its place when the door is closed. Some locks come with longer latches to make jimmying more difficult. Locks with latches of half an inch or longer are made by Sears, Sargent, and Corbin. To better resist physical assault some locks are made of pressed steel rather than the standard zinc casting.

Mortise locks: In general this type of lock offers more security than the key-in-knob lock because its locking mechanism is within a metal enclosure mounted inside the door, instead of in the knob. These locks have two locking devices, a convenience latch that keeps the door closed when it is slammed shut, and a deadbolt which you can lock

You can replace your standard key-in-knob lock with a decorative model like the Calcutta, a richly-beaded brass lock, handcrafted by Schlage.

Model depresses the trigger bolt on the Schlage lock. When bolt is fully depressed it locks the latch into place, making it impossible to loid.

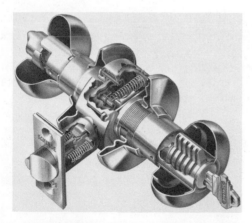

Cutaway of the Schlage Series B key-in-knob lock with deadlatching bolt. Note the keyway with five pin tumbler inside exterior knob.

Ornate lock designs for home or office can still provide good security (Schlage photo).

Many locks that provide extra security also present safety hazards. Not so with the Schlage Series G lock, which can be easily operated, even by a child. Both bolts will open when the child turns either the door knob or the thumb turn.

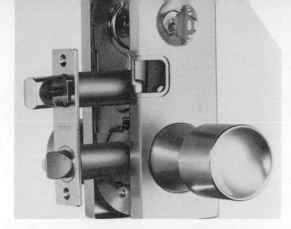

A deadlocking latch is combined with a rugged deadbolt in the Schlage Series G lock. Cutaway shows a concealed hardened steel roller in the bolt, which makes it virtually sawproof.

yourself by turning a knob inside the house, or by turning a key when leaving the house.

The major problem with this lock is not in its design, but in its misuse by the homeowner. Too often the convenience latch is used as the only locking device by the lazy or forgetful homeowner, who forgets to double lock the door when he goes to sleep, or when he rushes out of the house for the day. Any latch can be defeated in seconds by the loid user. Unless the homeowner remembers to use the deadbolt, this lock too, will prove almost useless.

Mortise locks vary in quality. When shopping for a mortise lock you should look for a lock that has a latch of about half an inch (longer if you see one) and a deadbolt which runs between 3/4 of an inch and 1 inch. The cheap locks have latches which barely fit into the door frame and bolts that are only slightly longer, making them easy to jimmy. However, some mortise locks come with protective faceplates which can be angled to minimize the distance between the door and the frame, making it more difficult for the door to be jimmied by a lock forcer.

Disadvantages of the mortise lock relate to the construction and installation of the lock. When mounted on a wooden door, the lock may actually weaken the door, because on narrow doors only a thin covering of wood lamination is left between the lock and the face of the door. With a good kick a burglar might be able to rip the lock out of the door. In addition, the lock cylinder is held in place by a single set screw on the faceplate of the lock. The set screw loosener, posing, for example, as a charity collector, will ring your doorbell. If you fall for his pitch you will ask him to stand by the door while you go inside to get some money. While you are doing that he will loosen or remove the set screw. At night he can return and easily pull the cylinder from the lock and get at the locking mechanism, releasing the deadbolt.

A solution to this problem is to look for a mortise lock that has a protective faceplate. Arrow, Yale and Sargent all make mortise locks with this feature as well as the adjustable angling plate which prevents jimmying. If you already own a mortise lock

Key cylinder is recessed into the faceplate of the Series G Schlage lock, making it less susceptible to wrenching. Knob on outside is free-spinning, so it can not be attacked with wrench or pliers.

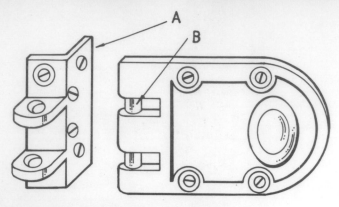

Vertical deadbolt lock. The lock is secured to the rim of the door with four long screws. Mating plate (A), is secured with between four and seven screws. Vertical deadbolt (B), secures firmly to mating plate.

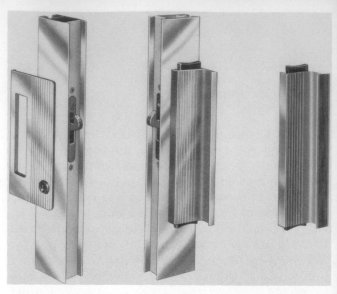

The unique Adams Rite bolt design, using a pivoted bolt, provides added strength for locking sliding doors. Note that all components are narrower than those on standard locks.

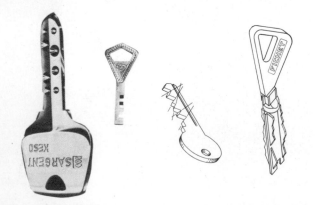

Unique design of the Fichet key makes it impossible to pick with conventional methods. Key control is accomplished by computer—only those owners who have received a factory-issued computer card can get duplicates of their keys.

High security keys—each operates a cylinder which is said to be pickproof. The Sargent Keso (left) uses a radial pin arrangement. The Abloy (second) relies on a springless cylinder core, working on a rotating detainer disc principle. The Medeco (third) incorporates V-shaped cuts which crisscross the key, providing millions of noninterchangeable key combinations. In the Fichet cylinder (right) each cut in the key is cut to ten possible depths and there are ten cuts, providing 60 billion possible combinations.

without a protective plate, you can protect it with either a dab of putty or bright nail polish placed over the set screw. Any activity, such as loosening or removing the screw, would be immediately evident to you.

Rim locks: these are really auxiliary locks. They beef up the security you get with your mortise or key-in-knob lock. They are mounted on the rim of your door about 6 inches above the primary lock, with the locking mechanism inside the house. The rim locks we recommend for the homeowner are those with vertical bolts which, when fitted into a mating plate, resemble a door hinge and pin. The lock is heavy-duty, as is the mating plate. Because the lock is installed with four long, heavy screws and the mating plate with four or more screws, it is virtually impossible to force from the door. And in fact, the standard jimmying tactic of putting a crowbar between door and frame does nothing to separate the lock from its mating plate or the door from its frame. Models are available from Eagle, Sears, Yale and New England Lock & Hardware (Segal locks), to name a few.

When you buy a lock it comes already assembled. Many people do not realize that the lock and the cylinder are two separate entities. A cylinder can be removed and replaced without replacing the entire lock which would, of course, be more costly. Some locks that are almost impervious to physical attack, may have cylinders that are easily compromised by the pickman. Ask your locksmith to tell

Installed in a sliding door, these locks by Adams Rite prove that locking hardware need not be ugly to be effective.

This Finnish-made Abloy deadlocking rim lock is made of rugged steel and brass. Its cylinder relies on a unique principle that supposedly makes it impossible to pick.

you which of your lock cylinders are easy pickins', and ask him to change them for you.

To understand what a cylinder is and how it can be picked easily, let's look inside one. Most modern cylinders have tumblers consisting of five small pins. They are arranged so that the notches in your key move the pins into a position that allows the core of the cylinder to turn and the lock to open. The pins are actually divided into two pieces and held in place by springs. The lower pins fit into the notches of your key. Because the pins are all different sizes, various depths are cut into the key to correspond to each pin—the longer the pin the deeper the cut. When you insert your key the pins line up at a point known as the shear line. In layman's terms the shear line is the point where the separation between the top and bottom pins allows the core to rotate within the cylinder and drive the bolt of the lock.

The pickman with his pieces of metal and tension wrench tries to accomplish with his equipment what you accomplish with your key. He lines up all of the pins with the pick and then turns the core with his tension wrench. He can be slowed down to some extent by cylinders which have mushroom-shaped pins. They are designed in such a way that if a pick rather than a key is used, the pins will jam in the cylinder. High-security cylinders are available which operate on variations of this principle and are extremely difficult to pick. The Sargent cylinder, for example, has three sets of cylinders

The Ultra 700 deadbolt is designed for easy installation. A template provided with the lock makes cutting a door cutout simple. The lock slides into the cutout and is secured by two screws. A faceplate protects the two screws.

arranged radially within the cylinder. The burglar will most likely not try to pick three sets of pins, a more difficult procedure than picking three standard locks. Duplicate keys are available only from the factory, making it difficult for a burglar to obtain your key. Medeco's cylinder has six pins which operate by a twisting principle instead of the normal alignment principle. Abloy cylinders, which fit only Abloy locks, rely on a rotation principle which has little to do with the standard pin tumbler arrangement. And Fichet cylinders utilize a ten-lever system which has yet to be defeated. Duplicate keys are available only from the factory and their issuance is controlled by a computer.

Many cylinders can be pulled out of the door with a large, heavy set of pliers unless they are flush with the door, or protected by a tapered cylinder ring. The cylinder puller need merely get a grip on the cylinder with his pliers and wrench it from the door. If the cylinder is tapered, thinner at the top and wider at the bottom, it is diffiuclt for the burglar to get a firm hold on it. Protective cylinder plates are available which cover the cylinder and the area around it, leaving only space for the key.

DECIDING WHEN TO USE WHICH LOCKS

The choice of locks available to you is almost limitless. You can use one or several to keep out the casual burglar. In New York we often see apartment dwellers with four or five locks. While this will slow down the burglar, it is not the solution to your problem. If the burglar has decided that he wants to get into your house because the potential rewards are great, he will spend whatever time is necessary to break down your defenses. And using five locks leaves a lot to be desired aesthetically, unless of course you are a hardware dealer.

Primary Locks

Both the mortise and key-in-knob-locks are called primary locks because they are the locks that usually come with your home or apartment. Although your builder would deny it, most of the

locks he puts in are intended to keep the door shut and do very little to keep the burglar out.

If your house has not yet been completed by the builder, or if you are building your own home, you would probably do best installing a mortise lock, remembering of course, its inherent weaknesses. If you are starting out fresh you should purchase a mortise lock that has both a protective faceplate for the set screw and an angling plate to minimize the distance between the door and the frame. Models of this type are produced by Sears, Yale, Sargent and Taylor. If you do not get these features you will be inheriting the weaknesses of the mortise lock which, quickly repeated, include: easy removal of the cylinder by the set screw loosener, and a susceptibility to jimmying because the homeowner most often does not remember to deadlock the door, relying only on the convenience latch. A mortise lock that overcomes the problem of misuse by the homeowner is manufactured by Abloy. The convenience latch cannot be locked and unlike other mortise locks you can set the bolt to close automatically when the door is slammed. Abloy cylinders are extremely difficult, if not impossible, to pick.

As a general practice, we don't recommend key-in-knob locks even though they are generally easier to install than mortise locks. The one exception is the Schlage Series G key-in-knob type lock. This lock has both a latch that extends about half an inch and a bolt that extends an inch. As a protection against physical assault the key is actually on the faceplate instead of in the knob, where it is likely to be subject to physical assault.

If your builder installs a standard key-in-knob lock, insist on one that is made of pressed steel, rather than zinc casting, in order to protect it from physical assault. Make sure it has a trigger bolt to prevent loiding. And make sure you get a latch that extends at least half an inch.

Every door in your home should be equipped with a good primary lock. Unless you use a Schlage series G or Abloy mortise lock, which fall into a different category than either the ordinary mortise or key-in-knob locks, it is essential that you add another lock for security rather than consider the economics or esthetics involved.

INSTALLING A NEW LOCK

a. *Remove worn out, broken, or low-security lock.*

b. *Lock may also be this type rather than that pictured in (a).*

c. *Remove latch of old lock.*

d. *Use template packed with new lock to mark area to be enlarged.*

e. *If a jig is available (as shown), use hole saw to enlarge area to accept new lock mechanism.*

f. *If hole requires only minor enlargement use a wood rasp or similar tool.*

g. *Cut away excess wood in edge of door, if necessary, to accommodate new latch plate.*

h. *Install latch.*

i. *Insert lock mechanism from outside of door.*

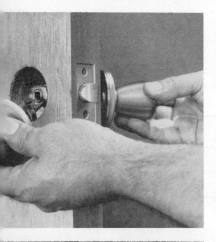

Secondary Locks

Because they are added on, they are known as secondary locks, but in terms of the security they provide, they are really the primary lock. They range from the vertical deadbolt, to locks which brace the door into the floor or deep into the door jamb. To decide which lock you need you should first examine the physical condition of both the door and the frame.

Metal doors or strong wooden doors and frame can probably be best protected by the vertical deadbolt lock, generically known as the Segal lock. Described earlier in this chapter, the vertical deadbolt lock offers excellent security, because with proper mounting it is usually at least as strong as the door itself. The burglar may actually have to tear down the door to get into your house if you use this type of lock. To get this lock at your home supply center or large hardware store, ask for a jimmyproof deadlock.

Another lock good for metal doors is the Abloy mortise lock. It is made of high quality materials

and is said to be nearly pickproof. Again, it adds strength to the door.

Wooden doors that are thin, poorly constructed, or rotting present special problems. If you install a good lock you may find that the burglar finds it easier to tear down your door than to force the lock. Therefore before you make any decisions, examine your door thoroughly for:

(1) Design. Is it solid or hollow? Does it have thin wooden or glass panels?
(2) Thickness. It should be at least 1-3/4 inches thick and made of hardwood.
(3) Deterioration. Is your door in good condition? Has the door rotted or weathered in any places? Has the frame rotted?

If your wooden door is in good condition you can use any of the secondary locks already described along with a solid primary lock, though we recommend that you reinforce the door frame with a strip of metal. Seeing a lock that he recognizes as tough to pick or break, the burglar who has

j. *Attach mounting plate on inside of door and snap on trim and knob.*

k. *Installation completed. This lock combines the security of a deadlock latch, with panicproof safety, allowing immediate exit with a twist of the inside knob (Schlage photos).*

decided he must gain entry to your house may start chiseling away at your frame until he creates a passageway for the bolt to be slipped through. While this is unlikely, you should ask yourself just how attractive your house is to a burglar. If the answer is "very," you need a reinforcing strip of metal.

If your wooden door is not in the best condition there are still a number of locks which will prove successful in keeping the burglar out without requiring that you replace the door. If your wooden door opens inward you might try the Fox Brace Lock, also known as the Fox Police Lock. This lock literally locks the door into the floor, operating in much the same way as a chair placed under a doorknob. A long steel bar which fits into the lock body (mounted on the door) rests in a metal socket in your floor. The floor bears the weight of any physical attack and is unlikely to give way. A good cylinder on the outside provides adequate protection from picking. In operation, locking the door from the outside moves the steel bar into a metal receptacle which prevents the bar from moving. Unlocking the door moves the bar within the metal receptacle (or lock body) to a channel that is open on the top and allows the bar to slide freely.

The lock is relatively inexpensive and is quite easy to install yourself with instructions supplied by the company. Its only drawback is its looks. However, you can remove the steel bar when you are at home and store it in a closet. Another excellent although expensive lock is the Fichet Vertibar which bolts into the door frame in seven places. Its protection is unparalleled.

For wooden doors that open outward the Fox double bar lock is probably the best. To overcome even the weaknesses of the oldest doors, this lock has two horizontal bars that extend from a centrally mounted case about two inches into each door jamb. In essence this takes the stress off the door and redistributes it within the door jamb. A similar recommended lock is the Sargent & Greenleaf Baricadeer.

Any of these locks can be used on a wooden or metal door. But a lock that has a short latch or deadbolt should never be used on a door that fits poorly into its frame. If your frame fit is poor,

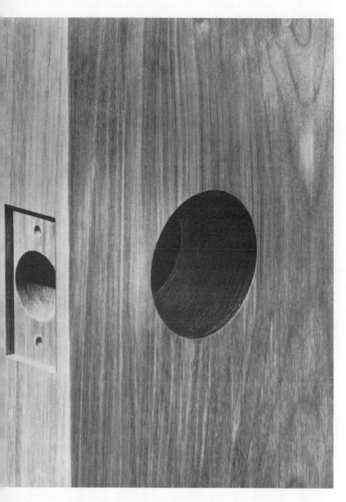

Typical preparation of a new door for installation of a standard key-in-knob lock. Templates provided for all new locks make lock installation an easy job for the do-it-yourselfer.

get a bolt of at least an inch. If the frame is rotting, use a brace lock, the Fichet Vertibar, or a double bar lock.

Special Problems

Sliding glass doors

As mentioned earlier, many people consider glass doors to be glass walls, and think little of their security. Also, the frames of the doors are so narrow that it is difficult to place lock hardware inside them; they provide little room for the installation of a bolt that is long enough to provide good protection. There are a number of inexpensive locks available for these doors. Loxem, for example, makes a low cost, lightweight lock consisting of a cylinder-operated deadbolt. Because it is lockable only from inside the home, some homeowners find this lock a bit inconvenient. However, its great advantage is that it can be easily installed and comes with tamperproof screws. This prevents the lock from being removed even if the burglar cuts a small hole in the glass to try to get at the lock.

For heavier duty security applications we recommend locks produced by Adams Rite. They are extremely narrow and employ a unique bolt design. The bolt is pivoted. When not in use it lies vertically within the lock housing. When locked, the bolt pivots to a horizontal position, providing the added security of a long bolt.

Swinging glass doors

These can also be protected by the Adams Rite lock, by some locks supplied by Loxem, and by several mortise locks designed for this purpose.

Garage or cellar doors

Padlocks are usually needed on these doors. The variety is endless, but many padlocks are too flimsy to be used for this purpose. Abloy, American, and a few other companies, however, supply some excellent, strong padlocks. You can get those that are key-operated or combination-operated. If you get a key padlock make sure it has a good tumbler, one not easy to pick. Buy the best padlock you can afford. Hasps are used to secure the padlock to the door. The hasp must be strong. Flimsy hasps are often broken by burglars who combine their strength with that of a crowbar to break off the hasp. If the screws that mount the hasp are exposed you should use nonretractable screws. Some hasps have a locking bar which conceals the screws when closed.

Using a padlock has its own special problems. If you are spending the day working in the garage, chances are that sometime during the day you will go into the house for a moment, leaving the padlock open. A burglar passing by can look at the type of padlock you have and then buy one which matches it. While you are inside your home he can replace your padlock with his. When you close the garage for the day you will be closing his padlock. At night he returns and inserts a key or uses the combination he knows. To make matters worse he may leave his padlock on the door so that you cannot open it the next day. To prevent this type of burglary you should put a dab of paint on the lock so you can recognize it. Or even better, never leave a padlock open. But if you find the lock has been replaced, call the police. They may be willing to stake out your house to catch the burglar. If not, cut off the burglar's padlock and replace it with a new lock.

Many padlocks come with code numbers imprinted on them so the locksmith will know which keys open them. Need we say more? File the number off the lock, and if you want, keep the number locked in a safe place.

Specialty Locks

You can get locks with push buttons, combination dials, or magnetic discs—all have no keyway, thereby foiling the lockpicker. But some have drawbacks of their own. They may be flimsy and fail when subjected to physical assault. If you use a combination lock you may forget the combination at some time. But the advantages can outweigh these disadvantages. Combination locks come in dial or push button models, with push buttons being the more widely used. Those most readily available are Simplex and Preso-Matic. Both are recommended, but Preso-Matic locks provide extra security at a low price. The locks have thousands of possible combinations, and it is said it would take several years of continual work to hit on the right combination on a lock with seven digits.

Some push button locks mount on the door rather than in it, in a large box. These usually fall prey to physical assault and cannot be recommended. However, a good lock like the Preso-Matic, which mounts inside the door, is extremely strong. In fact in a ghetto housing project vandals used sledge-hammers to try to break the lock and get through the door. Eventually they succeeded in jamming the bolt in the door jamb. But they could not get through. The major disadvantage to this type of lock is that it can be "read" over your shoulder. If a deliveryman follows you to the door with a package he may see the combination. Or a burglar sitting 50 feet away in his car might be able to observe you through binoculars. All we can recommend is that you block your actions with your body when opening the lock.

Magnetic keyless locks are not yet widely available. They have no keyway, instead relying on a small, round, half-dollar-sized disc, coded with small magnets. When the magnets in the disc align with the magnetic field in the door the door knob can be turned. The Alarm Lock from 3M is designed to foil the pickman, the loid user and the lock forcer. It is an auxiliary lock that sounds a siren if a burglar inserts a picking tool but fails to open the lock in four seconds, or if there is pressure exerted on the bolt mechanism or the guard chain. The alarm, powered by penlite batteries, may be loud enough to scare away the burglar. But unless you live in an apartment house it will not alert your next door neighbor.

If you go in for high security with a fairly high priced tag, you might consider the electric combination lock. The electric combination locks have a digital keyboard which can be mounted on or nearby the door. When the proper buttons are pushed, the door will open. A good electric lock is the Codetronic, by Sargent & Greenleaf.

More elaborate technologies will be widely available soon. Some day you will be able to open your door merely by saying a word into a device which is programmed to open the door only when it hears your voice. Or you might want to use a device that relies on hand geometry—the relation-ships of distances between different parts of your hand. Available from Identimation and in use in high security applications, the system has a reader which "reads" the characteristics of your hand and codes it into a special plastic identification card. If you wanted to get into your home you would place your hand on the same reader and insert the plastic card. The reader would compare your hand with the hand that was encoded on the card. If they matched, the door would open. Right now the unit in use is cumbersome, but in the future you will be able to place your hand on a spot in the wall which will read it, and then insert a card in a small slot next to it.

In the near future the widespread acceptance of these elaborate technologies will lower their prices drastically. Better and stronger locks will be available. So evaluate what your security needs are now and spend only as much money as is necessary.

Do I Need A Locksmith?

Most locks can be installed by the handy home-owner if he has a drill, a 1/4 inch drill bit, a hammer and some wood chisels. The advantage of working with a locksmith is that he can help you decide which locks you should use. He has a knowledge of the supply materials in your area and knows whether or not replacement parts are easy to get. Also, because he is called on to fix locks, he probably knows the most prevalent methods of breaking and entering in your town. If pickmen are abundant he will advise you to use a high security cylinder; if cylinder pullers lurk around every corner he will install a protective faceplate for the cylinder; and if brute force is the method most used by neighborhood thieves he can give you a lock that will resist physical attack. Of course, the greatest advantage of installing your own lock is the money you will save.

Key control

If you own your own home, only you and your immediate family members have keys that will open the door. But if you are constantly losing keys or leaving them at home you probably do what many homeowners do—hide the extra key under the doormat, in the bushes, over the door frame, or in any of the usual places. Even if you don't leave a key in these places regularly, there may be a time when you think you need to hide one.

Burglars would love to have the key to your house. That is why they look in all the usual places for that key. They may even see you placing a spare key under a doormat. They will take your key and either keep it or have it duplicated and replace it. So, don't ever leave a key outside your house; do not attach spare keys to the underpart of your car inside a magnetic case, and don't put your name and address on a set of keys. If they are lost the burglar knows exactly where to go. Burglars know all about these tricks.

If you do lose your keys, change the cylinder immediately.

APARTMENT SECURITY

Apartment security in many respects resembles home security. Because of the proximity of neighbors and the limited number of doors you must protect, you can save money by installing low-cost alarms that protect only one door or window. Although these inexpensive alarms do not produce enough noise to be used in private homes they can rouse neighbors in an apartment house.

The door to your apartment and the fire escape window are generally the only points of easy access. The window should be protected with a window gate. It need not interfere with room decoration as long as drapes are used to cover it, or an attractive protective device is chosen. Your door is vulnerable because often the superintendent and maintenance people have keys. In addition, past tenants may still have keys to your door. To protect yourself from the previous tenants install an auxiliary lock and keep it locked at all times, or have the cylinder on the existing lock changed. Make sure before signing your lease that you are allowed to take these security precautions.

In most apartment houses it is very rare that the superintendent or maintenance staff need to enter your apartment. However, it may be written into the lease that the maintenance staff must have a key in case they need to enter your apartment

during an emergency. You should protect yourself by doing one of two things:

(1) Give keys to your apartment to two trusted neighbors. Let the superintendent know who has the keys. In case of emergency one of your neighbors will probably be available to let the maintenance staff into your apartment.

(2) Ask your superintendent to keep your key in a sealed envelope. Explain to him that you trust him but that you know keys can be misplaced or stolen and that there is no way of being sure of the integrity of the janitorial staff. Seal the envelope yourself with a piece of tape and sign the tape so another envelope cannot be substituted for the original envelope. In case of a break-in ask for your key immediately.

The front door of the apartment building is perhaps the weakest link in apartment house security. In an apartment with sixty families there are probably two hundred keys circulating. A key is probably lost or stolen every week. Many apartments have buzzer systems for security reasons. To obtain entry a guest must buzz your apartment and speak to you before you open the electrically operated door. Unfortunately in many apartment houses the intercom system does not work and tenants are forced to buzz the door open for anyone who rings. This makes it easy for a burglar to get in the apartment house to look for an open door.

Demand that your landlord keep the intercom system in working order. Never buzz unless you know who your caller is. Never hold the door open for a stranger. Force him to use the intercom system to obtain entry. If there is a doorman he can be helpful in assuring that you are not hurt by a burglar or rapist. Ask your doorman to use the intercom to contact you several minutes after he sees you heading towards your apartment. If you do not answer, he should call the police. If the apartment does not have an intercom system there will probably be a phone by the doorman's stand. The doorman should phone you to make sure you are safe in your apartment.

Exchange telephone numbers with neighbors. If you see suspicious activity in the hallway, call your neighbors and let them know.

alarm systems

So far we have avoided talking about alarms, preferring instead to teach you how to make your home more secure structurally. Most of the methods already discussed should be used whether or not you decide to install a burglar alarm. And burglar alarms can be expensive—from $60 for a limited-use, home-installed alarm to a thousand dollars or more for an alarm installed by a large national organization and then connected to a central station monitoring point.

To help you spend your money wisely we will look at the purpose of alarms, when it is a good idea to have an alarm company install an alarm system for you, and how to go about installing your own system and saving a fortune.

PURPOSE OF ALARMS

While you probably think of a burglar alarm as a burglary deterrent—a device which will scare away the burglar and/or alert you to his presence in your house—police officers like to think of the alarm as contributing to the apprehension of those burglars who are not deterred from entering your home. Of all burglary deterrents, alarms are probably the most expensive. We already know that

locked doors and locked windows may be the best deterrents to crime. But even locked doors cannot keep out the burglar who has decided that the potential haul of goods from your home will be worth whatever trouble it is necessary to take.

Placing window decals on your doors and windows warning that the house is protected by an alarm can serve as an added deterrent, even if you do not have an alarm. The more-than-casual burglar, however, will look for external signs of your protection, such as an alarm bell, before deciding to pass up your house. Even then the determined burglar may try to get into your house. Remember, burglars can get past simple alarms. The inexpensive alarms, self-installed, will provide only a limited degree of protection. If you add auxiliary devices to them, however, you will have to increase your ante, but at the same time you will boost the quality of the system measurably.

What happens if the burglar still decides to attempt a burglary at your home? Although police like to think that with a good alarm, activated by the thief's attempt at entry, they will be able to catch the burglar, the key factor is how quickly the police respond to your alarm signal. If the police are cruising nearby and arrive within 30 seconds of the alarm signal, the police claim there is a 100 percent probability of capturing the thief.

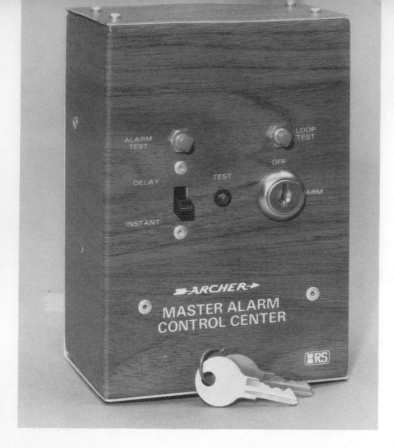

Typical scope and application of various components of the Archer Security system, supplied by Radio Shack.

SCOPE AND APPLICATION OF SECURITY SYSTEM

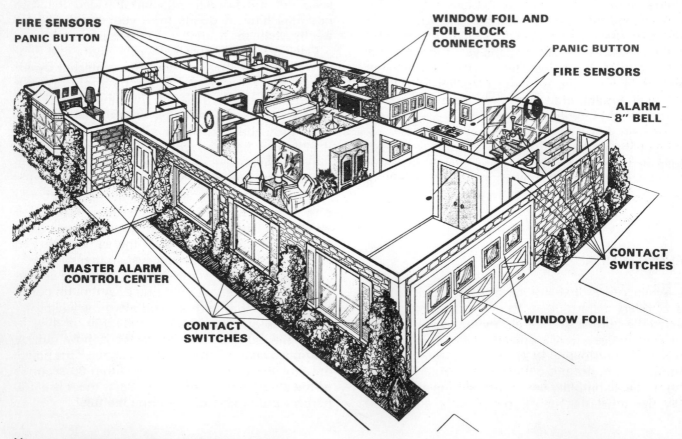

You can connect any number or type of sensors to this Archer alarm system, available from Radio Shack. Unit features choice of instant or delay modes, as well as an automatic reset after two to two and a half minutes. One of the lowest-priced alarms available, it sells for $29.95.

Similar statistics follow for different response times:

60 seconds	90 percent
2 minutes	75 percent
4 minutes	50 percent
10 minutes	20 percent

Of course the figures will vary in different localities, depending on how thorough the police are in searching for the burglar and on the area itself, which may provide some easy-to-reach hiding spots for the burglar. And, of course, a major determinant of the response time is whether the alarm that sounds a large bell outside your home is basically intended to scare away the thief—or whether it sounds instead in the office of an alarm company or police department. Use of a silent alarm can give police the added time they need. If the alarm sounds in their own office they can dispatch units to your house immediately. And the burglar, unaware that an alarm has sounded, can be caught inside your home. However, if you and your family are asleep inside the house you would probably be happier with an alarm that scares off the thief and signals the police or an alarm company at the same time.

Before looking into the proper methods of using a burglar alarm to protect your home and family we will look at the basics of an alarm system; how it works, and the different types of alarms available.

Doors can be protected with a nipple or pushbutton-type switch. When the door is closed the switch is pushed in; when it opens, the button pops out, triggering the alarm (Westinghouse photo).

ALARM BASICS

All alarms, from a $5 alarm that protects only one door, to a $2,000 system that protects a large home and signals the police, consist of three basic parts:

(1) Protective circuit—whether it is made up of wires connected to sensors, or soundwaves that blanket an area, its only purpose is to detect entry into a protected area.

(2) Control instrument—receives current from the protective circuit. If there is a change in

This external speaker from Delta products is attached to a siren module which transmits a loud, screaming noise to alert neighbors when connected to an alarm system.

Outdoor protection of a large building site can be accomplished with this infrared intrusion detector from Arrowhead Enterprises, Inc. The system has a range of up to 1,000 feet and uses invisible light. A burglar is not likely to be able to bypass this system.

the current, the control instrument activates the signalling device.

(3) Signalling device—issues a warning signal. A bell or siren goes off outside your home, or a signal is transmitted over telephone lines to police headquarters or some other central receiving service.

Generally the protective circuit is a constant electrical current which comes from a power source (batteries or house current), goes through the control device, passes through one or several intrusion detectors located at probable points of entry, then returns to the control device, completing the electrical loop.

Intrusion detectors are actually switches. When the switch is activated by an illegal entry it will either send or stop sending current to the control device which then activates the signalling device.

The control instrument is often called the "brain" of the alarm. It may be a complicated electronic device, but it operates on a simple principle. Whenever it receives an electrical signal or suddenly loses the electric signal, depending on the system, it activates the signalling device. It is the signalling device that determines whether the alarm is a local, central-station, or dialing alarm.

Local Alarms

This system generally has either a large and very loud bell, or a screeching siren as its signalling device. The signalling device is usually installed high on an exterior wall of the house. The bell should be heard for at least 400 feet. Some local systems come equipped with a self-contained signalling device, usually within the control device. This device, often a loud horn, is intended to alert the occupants of the house and perhaps to scare off the burglar. However, the signalling device should always be supplemented with a loud exterior bell. Of course if you live in an isolated mountain cabin the local alarm system may not be for you.

When a protected circuit is interrupted the bell rings either indefinitely or for a fixed period of time, perhaps five minutes, before it shuts itself off. In a densely populated residential area the best device is one that will shut itself off after several minutes. Within a few minutes of hearing the bell

SECURITY SYSTEM is composed of individual PLUG-IN UNITS with NO
…BLE MEANS OF CONNECTION from one to another. The secret is a highly
…nisticated method of transmitting the alarm signal from one component to
…her over the AC wiring of the building.

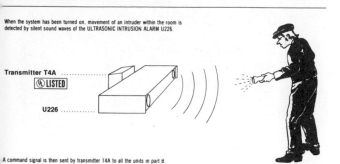

When the system has been turned on, movement of an intruder within the room is detected by silent sound waves of the ULTRASONIC INTRUSION ALARM U226.

Transmitter T4A …………

LISTED

U226 …………

A command signal is then sent by transmitter T4A to all the units in part B.

THE ALARMS ARE ACTUATED

Switched Receptacle SR3A

LISTED

Flashes a light on and off near a window to alert neighbors

Buzzer B3A

LISTED

Sounds a warning in your bedroom to awaken you

Horn H3A

LISTED

Sounds a very loud pulsating horn in the center of the house to frighten intruders

Outdoor Horn OH3A

LISTED

Sounds a very loud pulsating horn outdoors to arouse the neighbors

…ANIC ALARM

LISTED

Added protection can be provided by P3A which also transmits to the alarming devices in Part B above (bypassing the ultrasonic intrusion alarm on-off switch).

Panic Alarm P3A

- Can be moved from room to room
- Is actuated by momentarily depressing the hand held switch (turned off by pressing again)
- Actuates all items in Part B

…eration of a wireless burglar alarm system produced …Functional Devices.

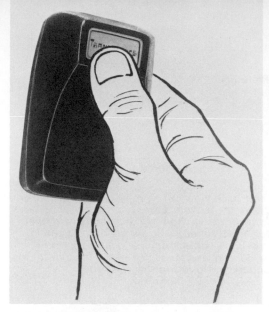

Pocket-sized transmitters which activate wireless alarm systems can be carried with you in your house or yard. If a prowler surprises you, you can sound an alarm even if the system is not switched on.

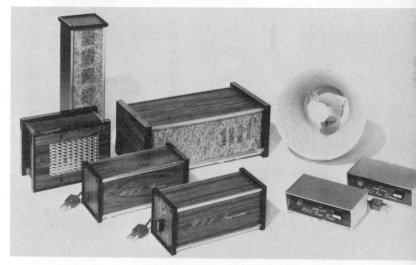

Everything from fire detector to ultrasonic intrusion detector is included in this wireless system from Delta Products. In operation, all devices are plugged into normal outlets and alarm signals are transmitted over house wiring to the external horn.

You can signal emergencies between any two telephones with the Dial & Coder from Delta. The unit attaches to any telephone and can be activated by many types of contact switches or by an ultrasonic detector. When the device is triggered it dials a preprogrammed telephone number and delivers a prerecorded message.

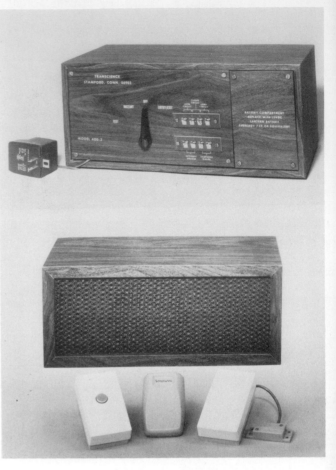

Front and back views of the Transcience wireless burglar alarm. System accepts a variety of sensors including: (from left to right, and bottom) a heat detector, a personal panic switch and magnetic contacts. Each contact device includes a small radio-wave transmitter which sends a signal to the control device triggering the alarm bell.

Typical photoelectric alarm system consists of a lamp unit and a receiver. Combining these units with mirrors will yield protection for large areas of your house.

 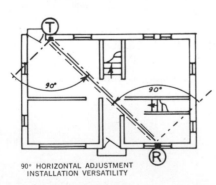

Arrowhead's solid-state infrared photoelectric system consists of a transmitter and receiver designed to look like a receptacle outlet. It transmits an invisible light beam up to 150 feet. Any interruption in that beam sounds an alarm. Mirrors can be used to bend light to provide protection in several rooms.

your neighbors will call the police or the burglar will be frightened away. Continued sounding of the bell only serves as a nuisance.

The major fault of local alarms is that very often neighbors will ignore the alarm, unless of course you have specifically asked them to notify the police when they hear the alarm. But usually neighbors are either indifferent or ignorant about the operation of an alarm. Either they don't want to get involved, or they think the sounding of the alarm is enough to alert the police. Often they will call only if the alarm has been sounding continuously for half an hour or so, disturbing their sleep. And of course by that time it is too late to do any good.

Central-Station Alarms

This system connects your alarm's protective circuit directly to a private organization which monitors a control panel with many alarm indicators on it. The signal reaches the monitoring panel by way of a leased telephone line set aside solely for transmission of alarm signals. The private organization that monitors the control panel, usually the company that installed your alarm, relays information to the police. Often the company has its own guard force and may send a guard to check on any alarm conditions.

The cost of the system depends on the size of your house and the complexity of the installation. In addition there is a monthly charge for maintenance of the leased telephone line.

Telephone-Dialing System

This system uses an automatic telephone-dialing unit with prerecorded tapes as its signalling device. When the control box signals an alarm situation this unit, which is attached to your telephone, starts dialing one or several programmed numbers and

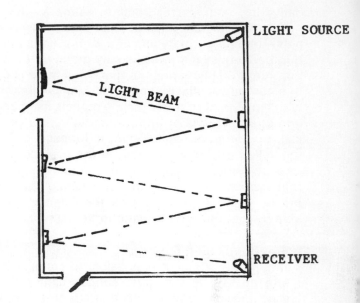

Intruder alarm from 3M works on the ultrasonic principle. Attractive cabinet design allows you to unobtrusively place it in any room.

Two methods of using photoelectric alarm systems are shown in these diagrams. In the top illustration, mirrors and a light source combine to web the room with a protective circuit. In the diagram below, two mirrors are used to extend coverage to an entire house by protecting a common hallway.

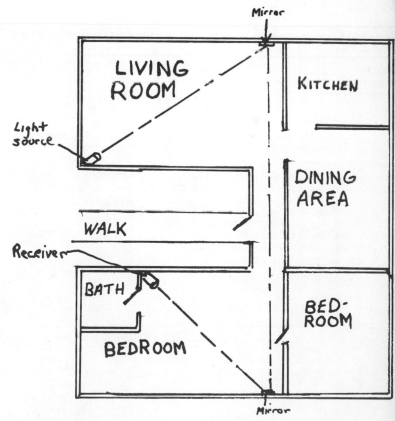

delivering your prerecorded message to the listener. Most dialers have at least 2 separate channels—one for burglary and one for fire. If the phone number is busy the units usually go on to the next programmed telephone number, or, if there is only one number, re-dial that number. Many units come with tape loops so the message repeats itself again and again. This is of importance in case a phone call is made to the police station, for example, and the call is put on hold because the desk sergeant is busy. When he picks up the phone again, the unit may be in the middle of playing the tape, but by staying on the phone the listener will be able to listen to the message in its entirety.

Police-Connection Systems

In some localities it is possible to connect your alarm directly to the police department through leased lines. Despite the fact that many local police officials are getting annoyed at the number of false alarms they must respond to, they still admit that

direct connection can be the most effective method of capturing burglars, because it reduces to a minimum the time needed to dispatch patrol units to your home.

WHAT KIND OF PROTECTION DO I NEED?

You can protect your house with: perimeter protection, area protection, object protection, or a combination of any of these three. Each requires a different kind of sensor and each offers a varied degree of protection.

Perimeter Protection

Your doors, windows, and even your walls, make up the perimeter of your home. Obviously, your main desire is to keep the burglar outside the perimeter. This can be accomplished in part by the use of fences or other barriers. Once the burglar gets into your yard you could detect his presence

About the size of a table-model radio, the 3M Intruder Alarm guards patio doors, windows and hallways with high frequency soundwaves. The unit turns on a lamp and sounds a siren if an intruder disturbs the wave pattern covering a 300 square foot area.

with ultrasensitive detectors that respond to light footfalls on your lawn, or you could use a system that fills your yard with a dozen infrared beams and sounds an alarm if the beams are broken, but these are out of the reach for most homeowners. As far as alarm protection goes you want to spend your money protecting the perimeter of your house and keeping the burglar away from your family.

In effect, a perimeter alarm system puts a protective electric fence around your house. If someone tries to climb that fence an alarm sounds.

The basic perimeter system is simple. It consists of sensors on doors and windows. They are most often magnetic switches. Each switch has two parts—an actual switch device sealed in plastic, and a magnet, also sealed in plastic. The magnet is mounted on the door and the switch on the door frame. If anyone opens a door or window protected by one of these switches, an alarm begins ringing. Unfortunately these switches (especially those mounted in windows) are subject to compromise by burglars, as you will learn in the section on installing your own alarm. To better protect your windows you or an alarm installer can put special current-carrying alarm foil on the window. If the window is broken the foil rips and the current is disturbed, activating the alarm.

A more elaborate perimeter alarm is the photoelectric system. It operates on the same principle as many automatic supermarket doors. Stepping in the path of a beam of light breaks the circuit in the first instance, opening a door. In a home, breaking the circuit signals an alarm condition. The photoelectric system consists of a sender and a receiver. You can put the setup in front of a door or window through which a burglar is likely to enter. Of course, there is no guarantee you will pick the right entrance.

Most perimeter systems are wired from point-to-point, connecting all vulnerable spots in your house, namely, doors and windows. Even if an installer is doing it for you, this involves a lot of wiring. However, there are several systems available that require minimal wiring.

Ask your alarm installer for a system whose sensors attach to radio transmitters. These tiny self-contained units send messages for a short distance via radio waves to the control center, where an alarm condition is signalled.

A unique approach to the wiring problem was devised by Flashguard. Their system uses flash-type units mounted along a line of sight from the sensor to the control unit. In simplest form, disrupting a sensor triggers a flash which triggers another flash-like device mounted quite a distance away. The process continues until the signal reaches the control center and a bell sounds.

Or you can get a unit whose sensors are wired to special AC transmitters that utilize your house current to send the message to the control center. The installer runs the wire from the sensor to the nearest AC outlet, where it is connected to a special transmitter which uses your house wiring to transmit signals, just like a wireless intercom.

In remote communities the AC carrier system has an added advantage—the transmitters will send the alarm signal to a neighbor's house over standard power lines, assuming the same power company feeds both homes with power. This is great vacation home protection. If you are away, a neighbor can summon the police. And if you have a boat house or remote guest house you can install a transmitter there to send signals to the main house.

Closed Circuit Television

Another method of monitoring the perimeter of your house is with a closed circuit television (CCTV). In most common applications the camera would be mounted above both the front and back doors, and generally would be used to observe anyone who rings your doorbell. In a large development however, a centrally located guard may have television monitors for many homes and/or the streets. Unless this type of system comes with your house you probably will not want to spend the money to add one. But if someone in your house is disabled, you might want to combine a CCTV camera, an intercom, and an electrically operated lock so that the disabled person could monitor and open the front door when necessary.

Area Protection

Rather than, or in addition to, protecting the perimeter of your house, you may want to give

Area protection and perimeter protection are combined into one system by Racon. The microwave intrusion detector has a range of up to 100 feet. In addition, magnetic switches and mat switches can be hooked up to the unit to trigger the two-tone alarm.

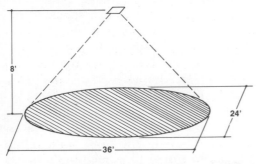

TYPICAL DETECTION PATTERN
Proportional to ceiling height

Typical detection pattern of a high-quality, ceiling-mounted microwave intrusion detector (Racon illustration).

added protection to the room where you keep your valuables. A highly sophisticated thief has less trouble with perimeter systems than with area-protection systems.

The variety of area- or space-protection systems is rapidly growing as available technology brings more space-age wonders down to the homeowner's price level. Right now there are at least six types of area-protection systems that can be purchased by a homeowner if he is willing to spend from $25 to $800. These include: photoelectric or infrared, microwave, ultrasonic, sonic, and audio.

While the photoelectric system was originally intended for perimeter protection, it can be easily made into a space-protection device. Photoelectric systems rely on visible light; however, more and more are starting to use invisible or infrared light. Whether visible or invisible light is used, the principle in area protection is the same as that in perimeter protection. If anyone breaks the light beam the alarm will sound.

In order to provide space protection with a photoelectric system you must set up several mirrors

Designed to resemble a high-fi speaker, this motion detector from Detectron has a range of about 50 feet. It operates on house current, but in case of power failure switches to its own power source.

BASIC HOME OR BUSINESS INSTALLATION

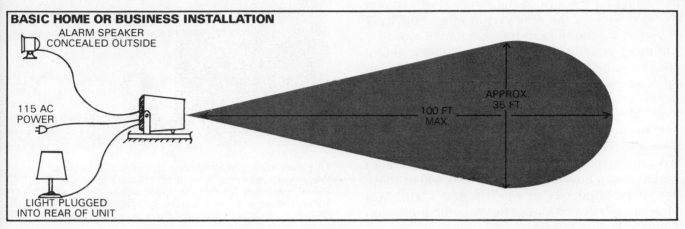

ALARM SPEAKER
CONCEALED OUTSIDE

115 AC
POWER

LIGHT PLUGGED
INTO REAR OF UNIT

100 FT.
MAX.

APPROX.
35 FT.

MAXIMUM PROTECTION INSTALLATION

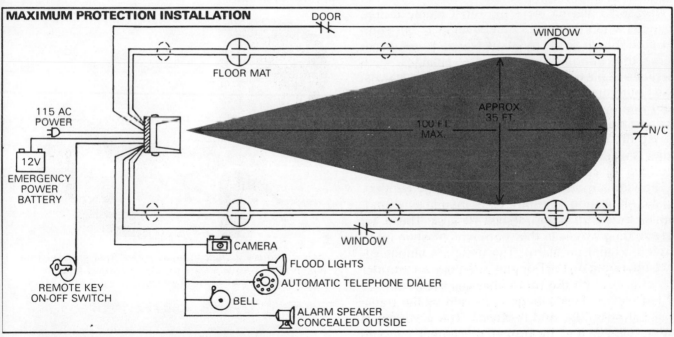

DOOR

WINDOW

FLOOR MAT

115 AC
POWER

12V
EMERGENCY
POWER
BATTERY

100 FT.
MAX.

APPROX.
35 FT.

N/C

WINDOW

REMOTE KEY
ON-OFF SWITCH

CAMERA

FLOOD LIGHTS

AUTOMATIC TELEPHONE DIALER

BELL

ALARM SPEAKER
CONCEALED OUTSIDE

*Two possible ways of using the Racon Microwave
security system. Unlike most motion detector systems,
this system also operates as a local perimeter alarm
system and allows hookup of a number of signalling
devices.*

in the room(s) you want to protect. Direct the light from the sender to a mirror on the opposite wall then to another mirror, back on the same wall as that of the sender but five or more feet away, depending on the size of the room. Finally, direct the light back to the receiver. In effect you have woven an electronic web throughout the room.

Infrared systems are better than straight photoelectric systems. Because the light is virtually invisible, it is nearly impossible for a burglar to avoid breaking the beam somewhere in the room at least once. Miniature units, with a range of about 50 feet, have been developed that fit into standard electric socket cutouts in the wall and are disguised to resemble the electric socket. A standard infrared system might have a distance of 250, 500 or more feet. With good use of mirrors and a standard infrared system you can perform home protection magic in several rooms.

Ultrasonic alarms were the most highly touted systems when they were first developed, but soon became known as the most overrated. It was discovered that various environmental changes, such as gusts of air from a heater, caused false alarms. Then burglars discovered that if they walked either very rapidly, or extremely slowly through the protected area, they would not set off the alarms of a majority of the systems. Like all new toys, their defects were repaired and they can now be recommended for area protection.

Ultrasonic motion detectors operate by continuously blanketing a room with inaudible soundwaves in the 18,000 to 45,000 Hz area. These set up standing waves in the room which, when interrupted, trigger an alarm. The units are ultrasensitive, operating on the Doppler principle. An intruder passing through the room changes the frequency of the waves. This change is sensed by the transducer (transmitter and receiver). The coverage is cone shaped, and by proper placement you can make it nearly impossible for a burglar to intrude upon the space you are protecting. Ultrasonic alarms are best suited for rooms without too much sound-absorbing material such as heavy drapes, carpets, or porous wall covering, because these substances reduce the range of the unit. Their sensitivity may also be affected by humidity. For

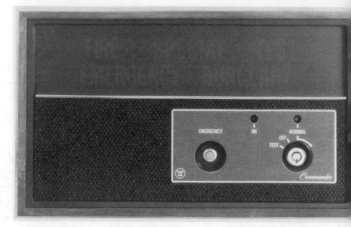

This decorator-styled control panel is the heart of the Westinghouse security system. The panel displays visual warnings for fire, burglary, emergency, test, and special purposes. Information is transmitted to a communications center, where it is relayed to the proper authority.

Westinghouse installer places cover over speaker unit which allows subscribers to talk to central-station personnel in case of emergency.

Competing for a larger share of the residential security market, Westinghouse has introduced an economy version of its standard central-station alarm system.

this reason it is important to check the alarm each time you set it. Conduct a test walk—walk through the room slowly. Take one step and stop. Take another and stop. If the alarm does not sound adjust the sensitivity. Repeat, running from one side of the room to the other. Again adjust the sensitivity if necessary.

An added benefit of the ultrasonics is that in many cases their manufacturers have made them to resemble books or stereo speakers, so that they can be placed unobtrusively in the room. The major drawback of ultrasonics is that pets, children, or sometimes a blast of heat from your furnace, may set off the alarm. Mice will also cause false alarms.

Microwave detection systems are similar to ultrasonic systems; the microwave- or radar-detection systems set up a pattern of standing waves, but they are electromagnetic rather than sound. Coverage may range from 25 to 70 feet. When it is first set up the unit receives reflected waves from the objects in the room as well as some direct waves from the environment. Once adjusted to the proper sensitivity, any change will sound the alarm bell. However, microwaves have some problems of their own. Their waves may pass through nonmetallic walls into the next apartment, the next room, or out onto the street. Careful placement will prevent most problems.

One manufacturer has available a system that overcomes the problems of both ultrasonic and microwave units by combining the two. Unless the unit detects a disturbance in both the microwave and the ultrasonic waves the alarm will not be triggered.

The sonic system is also quite similar to the ultrasonic system, and a little like submarine sonar. A sensitive receiver detects echoes coming from all objects in the room. If an intruder enters, the echo changes and an alarm is triggered. These systems are not yet widely available, but soon will be. They are said to be less susceptible to environmental influence than are ultrasonic systems.

As for acoustic alarms—sometimes called audio—you may have trouble finding a supplier at the moment. Even now they are in the $250 to $700 range. Instead of creating soundwaves, the audio-detection system listens for sounds. Microphones connected to an amplifier "listen in" on the protected area. If an unusual noise is detected an alarm will be triggered. They are subject to false alarms, but newer models have reduced the false alarm ratio.

Object or Point Protection

Whether it's a safe or a high-priced stereo system that you want to protect, you can add extra security

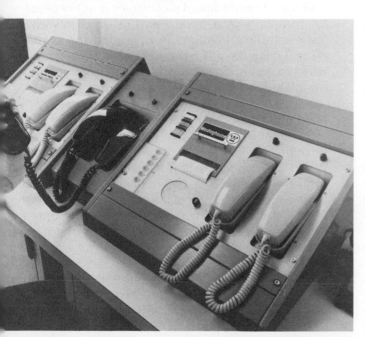

Trained guard personnel are on duty 24 hours a day to monitor signals from Westinghouse's central-station alarm system. One-way voice hookup allows you to explain nature of the emergency to the guard.

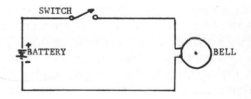

Typical open switch alarm circuit. Its operation is similar to that of a door bell.

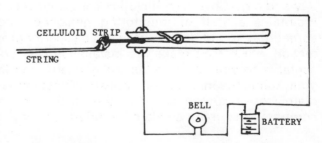

Diagram shows design of simple open-circuit clothespin alarm. Screws, screwed into clothespin serve as contacts. Celluloid strip separates contacts. If the string is pulled the strip will be pulled out, completing the circuit, causing the bell to sound.

through point protection. There are various methods of doing this. You can simply attach a leaf or bullet switch beneath the object you want to protect. Lifting the object opens the switch, disrupts the current, and triggers the alarm.

But for high-quality protection of an object—most often a safe—you need a capacitance detector or proximity sensor. In use, an electrical capacitor creates an electrostatic field around the object. The system works by turning the protected object into part of an electrical capacitor system. The electrostatic charge which is generated extends up to a few inches from the object. If the intruder approaches the object he interrupts the field and triggers an alarm. This is likely to scare him away before he can get a grip on your possessions. The system is costly—many installations run upwards of one hundred dollars per object protected.

THE ADVANTAGES OF HAVING AN ALARM INSTALLED FOR YOU

If you contract with a large nationwide company like ADT, you can be assured of getting exactly the system you want. An alarm specialist will help you determine which sensing devices you need and the best placement of these devices; in addition they will give you the cleanest installation because they are equipped with all the necessary equipment for stringing wires through your walls. An alarm specialist can evaluate the amount of protection you need on the basis of the value of your possessions and the attractiveness of your home as a burglary target. Of course, by applying the suggestions used in this book, you can do almost the same for yourself.

But by yourself you cannot connect your alarm to a central station, where it will be monitored day and night. The central-station company, which maintains a staff of monitoring personnel and sometimes armed guards, provides a superior protection which may make the installation cost acceptable to you. When a sensor is interrupted in your home, the interruption appears almost immediately on a control board at the central-station company. Generally an alarm company employee

will be alerted by both visual and audio signals. He will either call the police, dispatch armed guards, or both. Also you can choose from just about the most modern protection devices you can afford, from magnetic switches to photoelectric, infrared, microwave, or vibration detectors, all compatible.

If you choose a Westinghouse central-station system, there will be several panels located throughout the house which will allow you to communicate with the alarm company in case of an emergency. This allows you to signal even in case of medical emergency. And because you can explain the emergency to the monitoring personnel, you will get the help you need.

The average cost for monthly maintenance on central-station systems is about $30 (although ADT has a new system which lowers the cost considerably). An added benefit of central-station installation is that any malfunction in the system will cause a disruption in the circuit and the company will have a repair crew on the way to fix your alarm system immediately even if you are not aware there is any problem.

INSTALLING YOUR OWN HARDWIRED ALARM SYSTEM

While a knowledge of electronics is not necessary for installing your own alarm, a quick review of the electronics involved in operating the systems we will describe will help you make a better choice when selecting systems, and may help you pinpoint troubles you have when installing the system.

Normally Open (NO) Alarm Circuits

Switches in this type of system are in the open position, similar to a doorbell before you ring it. When they close, current flows to the battery and from the battery to a bell, causing it to ring. This is the simplest and one of the earliest configurations for an alarm system. Once the switch is opened the alarm will cease ringing. A sample of an open circuit alarm you can make to protect a gate or driveway follows.

Take a clothespin. Screw short metal screws into each arm of the clothespin, near the front. The screws should touch. Attach low-current electrical wire to each screw, preferably with solder. Attach one end of the wire to one terminal of a heavy-duty, lantern-type, six-volt battery. Attach the other end to one lead of a heavy-duty six-volt bell. Then run a wire from the battery to the other lead of the bell. The bell should sound. You have made a basic alarm circuit. Open the clothespin by exerting pressure. The bell should stop. You can use this type of alarm to sense heat or water, or to protect a driveway or gate.

To protect a gate: insert a piece of celluloid or a thin strip of wood between the two halves of the clothespin, separating the contacts. To that attach a thin wire. Set it up by attaching the wire to the gate in such a way that opening the gate will pull the wire, pulling out the celluloid and allowing the circuit to be completed. To protect a driveway from unauthorized cars or visitors entering it, string the wire about a foot off the ground across the driveway, and attach it to the garage so a car passing by would pull the celluloid out of the clothespin.

Tools required for installation of alarm system include: screwdriver, wire strippers, hand drill, hammer, soldering gun and solder (optional), electrical tape, 1/4 inch masonry drill bit, 1/2 inch masonry drill bits, and miscellaneous drill bits (Universal Security Instruments illustration).

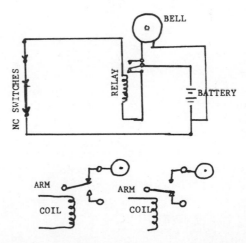

Typical normally closed alarm circuit. In diagram the relay is energized, holding the arm to the bell in an open position (illustrated in diagram, bottom right). When current falls out because of interruption to the circuit, the arm will spring into the closed position (bottom left), allowing current to flow to the bell.

Control panel for the ADT home alarm system is mounted inside the home, near an exterior door. Pushing a button before leaving the house activates the alarm. To deactivate the alarm a personal code must be indicated. If it is not, an alarm signal is silently transmitted to an ADT central station.

This self-contained unit protects doors from unauthorized entry. Any force exerted on the chain will cause the alarm to sound (Radio Shack photo).

If you want the alarm to detect a rapid rise in heat, put a small ball of wax which melts at a low temperature between the contacts. In case of a fire the wax will melt and the bell will sound.

To detect moisture: insert an aspirin between the contacts. You might want to mount this system in your pool, just above the water line. Use the system only when the pool is not in use. Put the tip of the clothespin just above the water line. If someone falls into the pool, the water will rise and dissolve the aspirin, and the bell will sound. You can also use it as a rain detector on a day that you want to air the house but are afraid the rain may come in through your open windows. Use the aspirin design again. Put the clothespin on your window sill. The aspirin should dissolve before the rainfall becomes too heavy.

Other types of open circuit detectors include some fire detectors, doormat switches, and bullet-type switches. The problems associated with a circuit of this kind can best be understood by looking at its principle of operation. Relying on an absence of an electrical signal, as it does, this system is subject to compromise simply by cutting any of the wires. Because the current flows only when the electricity completes a loop, removing any switch or cutting any wire will disable the system. Of course, mat-type switches which fit under your rug may not be detected by the burglar, and offer good protection.

Normally Closed (NC), or Closed-Circuit Systems

These are less susceptible to defeat than NO systems. The electricity constantly flows in a loop. Any interruption of current in this loop triggers the alarm bell. The secret of this type of system is a relay (a sort of magnetic switch), or an electronic switch similar to a relay. While energy is flowing through the relay the magnet is energized, holding a switch in a position which does not allow current to flow to the alarm bell. Interrupting the flow of current to the relay causes the switch to close, redirecting the current to the bell. This could be caused by breaking the contact on a sensor, cutting the wires, or by a malfunction in the system.

And unlike normally open circuits, the closed-circuit alarms are generally equipped with internal

MASTER CONTROL PANEL   SOLID-STATE ELECTRONICS

Universal's security system comes complete with six magnetic switches, heat sensors, panic switch and warning decals. The control box is intended for exterior mounting.

Many modern burglar alarms are compact, relying on solid-state electronics. This low-cost alarm from Kwikset can be mounted in a wall. Self-contained alarm alerts occupants to intrusion.

circuitry that keeps the relay from returning to a safe or off position. So closing a door he has opened, the burglar will not be able to silence the alarm. The only way he could silence the alarm would be to find the alarm control box and totally disable it. If an alarm sounds you can silence it by inserting a key into a switch in or near the control box and shutting it off.

Heat sensors are easy to add to your alarm system. They may be either normally open, or normally closed. A heat sensor may rely on a fuselike piece of metal which melts in case of a rapid rise in temperature—thus operating as an NC switch. When the metal melts, the circuit is interrupted and a bell will sound. Or a heat sensor might contain a thermostatic button which pops open at a certain temperature. In a normally closed circuit, the sensor would be designed so that the button would break a circuit when popping open. In a normally open circuit the button would pop open, making, rather than breaking, the circuit.

Some alarm systems are set up to accept both normally open and normally closed sensors, for added versatility.

The most commonly used sensor in alarm systems is the magnetic switch. It consists of two parts. One, the actual switch component, is made of two metal contacts a fraction of an inch apart, housed in plastic. The second component is a magnet, also mounted in a plastic housing. When the magnet is brought close to the switch it draws the two contacts together, completing a circuit. These can be mounted on doors or windows, even on desk or dresser drawers.

CHOOSING THE RIGHT SYSTEM

It is easy to install an alarm system, however there are several features to be considered which can make installation easier and improve your protection.

Key operated switch: If your control box is going to be mounted outside your house, as in many homeowner-installed alarm systems, it will come in a heavy, tamperproof box with a key switch. This allows you to activate or deactivate the alarm

Low-cost protection of a single door can be accomplished with Radio Shack's Powerhorn Jr. Spring activated plunger at top triggers a self-contained alarm. Unit costs less than $3.

You can design your own burglar/fire alarm system with these modules from Detectron. Various component boards form latching relays, electronic sirens, power supplies, and complete fire or burglar alarm circuitry.

Low-cost burglar alarm systems for homeowner installation come in a variety of styles. Most come in complete kits with all necessary components, wire, and easy-to-follow instructions.

Magnetic switches are the mainstay of nearly all burglar alarm systems. Top unit contains a switch which closes when a magnet, housed in the lower unit, is brought near it.

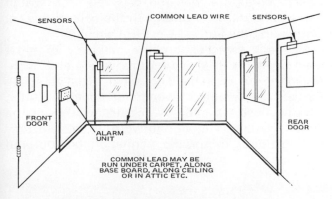

Typical illustration of wiring of components in an alarm system. Kwikset illustration.

system from outside the house. Other systems allow you to install the control box in the house and the key switch outside. In either case you should install the key switch higher than shoulder level, making any attempt to pick the lock more difficult.

Time delay feature: We highly recommend a time delay feature on your alarm. This allows the control box to be located inside the house. A 10 to 20 second time delay permits the homeowner to set the alarm and then leave the house. The homeowner has the same amount of time to reach the control box and deactivate it upon entering the house.

Normally open/normally closed feature: Some alarms come equipped with circuitry for both normally open and normally closed systems. This is desirable if you want to use devices other than magnetic switches as part of your total home protection plan. You can tie in mat switches, fire sensors and similar devices, as well as homemade sensors.

Flush mount or wall mount: Some alarms are designed specifically for mounting on exterior walls. They do not add to the beauty of your home. Alarms designed for interior installation may be mounted in or on the wall. If you have the time and the inclination, we recommend that you install your control device in the wall. This provides an added degree of protection from tampering, and gives the system a customized look.

INSTALLING SIMPLE ALARMS

The Powerhorn Jr., available from Radio Shack, is useful for apartment dwellers or homeowners who want a simple, inexpensive method of scaring the burglar and/or alerting neighbors.

The unit is a normally open, self-contained alarm. A spring-activated plunger acts as the switch. Install it on your door in such a way that when the door is closed it depresses the plunger. When the door is opened the plunger should spring forward and sound an alarm. The unit is simple to install, but only of limited use. It has a self-adhesive pad for temporary installation and two screws which are used for permanent installation. The drawback with this model is obvious. It sounds any time anyone opens the door—when you come home from a picnic, for example. So after a while neighbors tend to ignore it. And a burglar picking your lock or forcing your door can silence the alarm with a good hammer blow.

Radio Shack's Powerhorn Sr. uses a door chain as its triggering mechanism. If a prowler forces the door, the chain tightens, triggering the alarm. Other companies make similar alarms; the models described above were mentioned because of their wide availability.

If you do not wish to put a self-contained alarm on every door and window you will opt for either a hardwired alarm for perimeter protection, or an ultrasonic-type alarm for motion detection or area protection.

Hardwired Perimeter Alarms

Let's start with the alarm box and work outward for installation purposes. We will give you general instructions for installation as well as some manufacturer's instructions for widely available models.

Step number one is to decide upon the location of your control box. Control devices which are designed for installation on an exterior wall generally come in heavy-gauge metal boxes with tamperproof switches. Any attempt at opening the box will result in the alarm sounding. The control box most commonly has a key-operated switch. Install the box above shoulder level to prevent picking of the key switch, and mount it solidly on the wall by using anchors. Some manufacturers supply kits with all the necessary parts for alarm installation, however the alarm we bought came with only four standard screws for wall-mounting the heavy metal box.

Surface-mounted interior control boxes should be secured the same way, with anchors, to prevent the unit from being ripped out of the wall by intentional or unintentional misuse. Usually four screws, supplied with the unit, are partially screwed into the wall. The cabinet is then slipped over the screws and the screws tightened.

Some manufacturers, notably Kwikset, supply a surface-mounting bracket for their unit. By locating the adjacent studding near the door, you determine where to mount the unit. The bracket is then held

in the desired position while you mark the places for installation of screws. Once the bracket is secured, the unit slips onto the bracket.

For recess-mounting of control boxes manufacturers generally supply rough-in boxes. Locate the studding by sounding the wall or by using a stud finder. Templates supplied with the rough-in box show locations for drilling holes for anchors or screws. After all holes are drilled a cutout is made into the wall with a hacksaw blade or sabre saw. The unit mounts easily into this space. All exposed plaster is covered either by the faceplate of the unit or a trim panel, for a custom-installed look.

Wiring

Wire simply brings the circuitry from one point to another. If you plan on combining normally open and normally closed sensors you must keep the wiring on different runs of wire. Wiring can be glued to molding, run under carpeting or behind shelves, etc., to make it as inconspicuous as possible. This is most easily accomplished in a house still under construction. Wiring in existing structures should take advantage of all existing moldings and trim pieces. If you live in a straight-walled house with no trim at all, you can use a special wiring that is flat and need only be pressed into place. It can be installed to look like molding. U-shaped nails used by the telephone company or staples are also useful for installation of regular alarm wire. Use double-stranded wire for ease of installation. You can do all wiring yourself because it is low-voltage wiring, not covered by building codes.

Sensors in a closed circuit system must be wired in series. One wire goes from the power source or control box to the first terminal of the magnetic switch. Wires are then run between each switch and finally one wire returns to the control device, completing the loop of electrical circuitry.

Magnetic switches are the mainstay of most alarm systems. Both surface-mounting and flush-mounting are available. For ease of installation use the surface-mounted switch; for added security, use the flush-mounted switch. Installation of the surface switch is straightforward. If you are protecting a door, mount the magnet on the door and

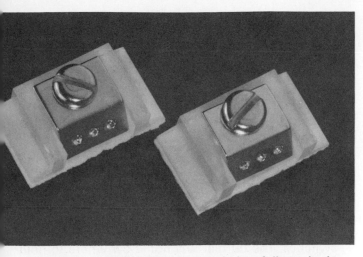

Adhesive-backed blocks connect window foil to wire in a hardwired system without the need for soldering.

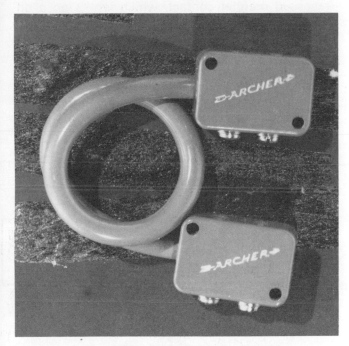

Door connector cords can be used on doors or windows. On windows they would connect the foil connector blocks to wire running from the window frame, allowing the window to open without breaking the wire.

the switch on the doorframe. The switch portion must be on the surface, which remains stationary because you will have to run wires to and from it. For best protection and attractiveness mount the switch at the very top of the door frame. This makes it more difficult for a burglar to attempt to defeat the switch, and the wires are easier to conceal by running them along the edge of the frame.

Use screws, glue, or double-sided tape if you get stuck. For the average wooden or metal doors, screws should be used to mount the sensors. For problem installations where there is no room for screws, you might want to glue the switch to the door or window.

Sensitivities of the switches vary. You should mount the two components as close together as possible, but sometimes you will have problems in doing so. On one of our doors we found that the molding did not allow clearance for the magnet and the switch. We had to mount the switch 3/4 of an inch from the magnet and on a different plane. If you have a similar problem, mount the components temporarily with tape and test the alarm system. If the alarm does not sound your magnet is strong enough to hold the switch contacts at that distance. Mount the contacts permanently with screws. Generally you can expect about 3/4 of an inch to be the maximum distance between magnet and switch on wooden doors. Metal doors seem to reduce this to as little as 1/4 inch.

Flush-mount switches are much smaller than the surface-mount type and are easy to conceal. Drill a hole at the top of the door, large enough to accommodate the magnet. If the door is steel, you will probably have to drill a slightly larger hole so you can insulate the switch with plastic. The switch portion is installed in a hole drilled in the door frame, immediately above the magnet. Wires can be fed through the frame, upwards and then alongside the frame. Or, if you have opened the wall to insert a roughing-in box, you can drill directly through the frame and thread the wires into the wall, toward the control device.

A problem we have found with some magnetic switches is that they can be defeated by a strong external magnet. In fact it was discovered that we

A good tool to have when installing long runs of wire is the Arrow stapling gun. Most types of wire will fit in the staple channel.

Self-sticking metallic tape is used on windows to carry the protective circuit. When the window is broken the tape breaks and the circuit is interrupted, sounding the alarm.

This panic switch is used for manual on-off control of alarm system in case of emergency.

could enter and leave a home without triggering the alarm simply by carrying a small magnet. We opened the door wide enough, without sounding the alarm, to place the magnet next to the switch and to tape it in place. We then went to the alarm box and deactivated it. Of course a burglar would not even have to deactivate the alarm. With the door open he could carry out his business and leave.

This is a good reason to use hidden magnetic switches. The burglar will not know where to hold his magnet. And if you are interested in a higher degree of security you might want to try Ademco's recessed magnet contact, which works on a different principle. In the Ademco switch two magnets are used—one in the door, and another in the switch component located in the door frame. When these are brought close together they repel each other, closing the protective circuit. The switch uses a "narrow beam magnetic field" said to be almost invulnerable to assault with an external magnet.

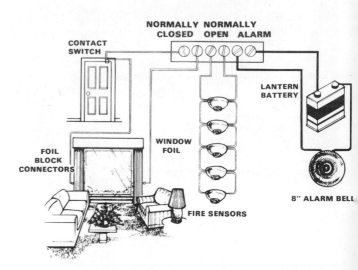

Diagram showing wiring of the Archer alarm system, available from Radio Shack. Note that all normally closed sensors must be mounted in series and all normally open sensors must be mounted in parallel.

WINDOW FOIL AND FOIL BLOCK

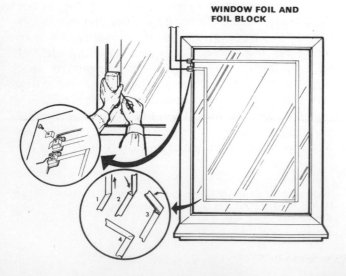

Window foil installation used in most alarm systems is illustrated using Archer alarm foil and foil block connectors. A wooden block is used as a guide for drawing guide lines around the window. Start the foil at an edge, leaving about two inches over the edge for later connection to the adhesive-backed connectors. When you come to your first 90 degree turn, lift the foil up and then back down over itself as illustrated. Repeat for all 90 degree turns. To assure good contact at turns, prick foil with a pin at least five times. Smooth out the foil with a matchbook cover. Wire the connector blocks into the system.

Window Foil

To prevent the burglar from smashing through your window, you need window foil. This foil is electro-conductive, carrying current like a wire. Most alarm kits come with a roll of the foil, or you can buy a roll at most electronics or large hardware stores. To install it, clean the window with alcohol or ammonia. Using a three-inch block of wood or cardboard to serve as a guide for laying of the tape around the frame, mark the window either with chalk, a felt tip pen, or a grease pencil, preferably on the outside. Start at the top of the window, in the corner where you will install a foil connector block. Some blocks have wire leads; if yours does, start the alarm foil over the lead. Lay the foil out slowly, rubbing it with a matchbook cover to keep it from wrinkling.

When you reach a point where you must make a corner, fold the foil back and then double fold it at the corner to keep the sticky side facing the glass. Pierce the corner four or more times with a pin or small nail to insure proper contact. Finally bring the foil back to starting point.

The leads of the connector block can be attached to the foil by either relying on the adhesive property of the foil (simply lay the contacts of the foil block beneath the foil), or using a cool soldering iron. Finally, install a door cord on the window frame to connect the foil on the window to the alarm circuit.

Other Triggering Devices

The only way to trigger the alarm with a panic switch in a normally closed system is when the system is already switched on. If you want, you can install an interior on-off switch, which overrides the key switch. Then if you hear a prowler during the day you can switch the alarm on and then press the panic button. You might want to place a setup with both switches in your kitchen and one at your bedside. Connect panic buttons in the same manner as you would magnetic switches. A better system is provided by an alarm that uses both NO & NC sensors, which allows the panic button to trigger the alarm regardless of whether it is on or off.

Most alarm kits allow you to wire fire sensors to the regular burglar alarm circuit. We do not approve of this method of fire protection. Fire sensors should sound a different horn than a burglar alarm, and that horn should be in the hallway near the bedrooms. We recommend, therefore, that you install a separate system, perhaps one of your own design, if you plan on using the standard heat-activated fire sensors.

But a much better method of protection for fire safety is installing a self-contained smoke- or products-of-combustion detector (PCD). These units can be mounted in your hallway near your bedroom and will give you an early warning. These units generally have a loud alarm bell or horn inside them, easily distinguishable from the burglar alarm. The PCD will alert your family long before a fire is a serious danger. The smoke detector takes a bit longer to operate, but is also recommended.

By following the instructions in the alarm kit you buy and by looking for the features we recommend, you can design an effective burglary prevention system. We recommend that you make a floor plan of your house to help you decide where to install various sensors and how to run the wiring.

low-cost security and community action

There are dozens of security measures you can implement with little or no money. All they involve is using some common sense and a touch of criminal sense. But before we describe some of the methods of safeguarding your home we want you to participate in a simple exercise.

Exercise: "Case" your house. Pretend you are a burglar who wants to break into your house. Take a walk out into the middle of the street to get a good overall view of the "scene of the crime." Now, plan your heist. How would you break into your own home? Find the weak points now and patch them up later.

If you don't take part in this exercise you will be doing yourself and your family a disservice. Purchasing all of the security devices under the sun will do you little good unless you become committed to overall crime prevention in your home.

Follow the outline below as we take you through an imaginary session in practicing criminal sense.

LIGHTING

First take a look at the street lighting. Is your neighborhood well lit or poorly lit? If an entire neighborhood is well lit it can keep the burglars away. How about your own house? How far are

you away from the nearest street light? Is the light obscured in any way? Too often street lights are installed in good positions only to have trees grow up and block their light. If this is the case, cut back the tree or trees. If your neighborhood is poorly lit, you should form a block or neighborhood association and develop a plan of action aimed at getting lighting improved by your local government.

Next, take a look at your own outdoor lighting. Too often there will be nothing to look at, because you have no outdoor lights. Install lights following these guidelines.

Front door: you should have a bulb burning brightly all night long. For garage doors and other entrances use smaller bulbs, 40 watt for example, but keep them on throughout the night to discourage the burglar. If you are on vacation you should purchase photoelectric devices which you can screw into each bulb socket. They will automatically turn the lights on when it gets dark and turn them off in the morning. In the yard, your front and backyards are outside perimeter defenses against the burglar. And if they are totally dark, or even partially shaded, they will offer the burglar concealment.

Unless you live in a new subdivision house where the trees are still small, there are bound to be some shady areas which will need special lighting. You can use lights mounted atop the house or at a distance from it. In order to provide illumination of the yard and the shrubbery near the house you will want to use lights mounted on a post at a distance from the house. You will discover that even with relatively good street lighting and the existing front and back door lights, a good portion of your yard and some of your house, remains in shadow. Use a wide-angle floodlight mounted far enough away from the house so it will eliminate shaded areas in your yard. These lights serve the added purpose of causing the burglar to cast a very large shadow. This is a good psychological deterrent. The only caution here is to secure the wiring for these lights in metal conduit so they cannot be cut by the burglar.

To eliminate the dark areas immediately adjacent to the house you will want to mount some spot or floodlights in a corner high atop the house. You can aim these lights so they cover a wide area of each wall. You might want to control these lights from your bedside so that when you hear a prowler you can turn on the lights and frighten him. If you have a burglar alarm system you can wire it up so that raising a window, or in any way attempting to break into the house will turn the lights on.

the expense of installing high-power floodlights, you should at the very least install a 40-watt bulb at each corner of the house, perhaps hanging from the gutter, and keep them burning all night. They will at least take care of the shadowy areas immediately adjacent to the house.

Interior Lighting

Your interior lighting can also serve as a defense against the burglar. A trick which is quite common but can be made to work, follows. Buy a timer for $5 to $7 and connect it to your bedroom light. You can set it to go on at 8 p.m. and off at 3 a.m. At first glance the house may appear occupied. But a couple of hours or a couple of nights will show the thief that the light goes on and off as regularly as clockwork. There is only one conclusion he can draw.

Solutions:

Buy four timers and set them in various parts of the house—living room, kitchen, bedroom and bathroom. This should cost you about $25 (less if the timers are on sale).

Choose a living pattern such as A, B or C in the table below.

	Living Pattern Table					
ROOM	**A**		**B**		**C**	
	ON	OFF	ON	OFF	ON	OFF
KITCHEN	6 p.m.	10 p.m.	7 p.m.	midnight	8 p.m.	1:00 a.m.
LIVING ROOM	7:30 p.m.	11 p.m.	8 p.m.	1 a.m.	8:30 p.m.	midnight
BEDROOM	10:30 p.m.	1 a.m.	midnight	3 a.m.	10:00 p.m.	2:00 a.m.
BATHROOM	11:00 p.m.	morning	11:30 p.m.	morning	9:00 p.m.	morning

The lights, which are mounted at a distance, can be combined with house-mounted lights. In some cases, the distant lights may cause glare, making it difficult to see a prowler. If you have house-mounted lights this will cancel out the glare of the other lights and make the prowler feel he is trapped in a gridwork of light. In any event if you decide that installing both sets of lights will fit into your budget, the burglar will take this as an off-limits sign.

Economy lighting: If you do not wish to undertake

The idea is to create a possible living pattern—to make the house look occupied with people moving from one room to another, sometimes leaving on lights in two rooms at the same time. Of course you can choose your own living pattern as long as you remember to overlap the times lights are on in at least two rooms. You will note that in each case the bathroom light is left on until morning. This is because it is easy for a burglar to believe that a family might leave the light in the bathroom on all night. You might also want to set the kitchen timer up to a radio which is tuned to a talky radio station.

And, of course, don't leave your drapes or shades wide open so a prowler can look inside to find out if anyone is home.

Another solution to the timer problem: With only one or two timers in place, ask a good neighbor to come by in the daytime and reset the timers every few days during the period you are away from home.

FENCES: REAL AND IMAGINED

For our purposes a fence is anything that delineates the beginning and end of your property. It is a tangible statement of your property line. A fence can be of chain links, bushes, or brick. Anything at all that separates your house and family from the rest of the world is a fence.

We are not suggesting that a three-foot high picket fence will make it impossible for a burglar to invade your front yard. However, fences serve as good psychological deterrents. When you put up a fence, you are, at the same time, putting up a signpost stating: "This is my property." You will notice that even children who think nothing of wandering into the front yards of homes which do not have fences will have second thoughts about entering a yard protected by a fence.

The same is true of the burglar. Psychologically, you have told him that you care enough about your property to keep people out. Legally you are telling him that if he jumps your fence he will be trespassing (in many states it is difficult to get a trespassing conviction unless property boundaries are clearly marked). For the casual burglar, this may serve as enough of a warning.

Of course not just any fence will do.

If you have a six-foot-high brick wall or hedge and are feeling safe, you shouldn't be. In fact you should head right out into your yard and cut that fence in half. The purpose of a fence is to make it more difficult for a burglar to get onto your property. A fence should not, at the same time, provide cover for the burglar while he conducts his business.

Let's look at some alternatives to the high brick wall or its associates—spikes and barbed wire.

A wooden picket fence is easy for a burglar to jump, but again, it serves as a psychological deterrent. Also, if your fence is no more than 40 inches tall it is still easy for neighbors or a passersby to see the burglar at work.

Install a gate—don't leave an opening—at the beginning of your walkway. If the burglar has the choice of jumping a fence or walking through a gate he will probably choose the latter. And if he does he will run into this simple security system which you can set up: Tie a cord to the gate. To the cord attach a string of tin cans, or preferably, a string of bells. During the day this serves as an annunciator, telling you someone has entered your yard. At night it has a small fright factor for the burglar, and may awaken you. Or you can rig up a simple electrical alarm to the gate, as described in the chapter about alarm systems.

Chain link fences make up in protection what they lack in beauty. If you feel the need for a six-foot-tall fence, then the chain link fence is for you. While allowing added height and acting as a good physical barrier, it does not obscure vision. Chain link fences are easy to install, but extra care should be taken by anchoring them into concrete-filled holes. Remember too that the fence must protect the area below it as well as the area above it. A one-foot space, no matter how small it looks to you, can easily be passed through by a burglar who is a professional squirmer. So keep the fence as close to the ground as possible. Again a gate is necessary at the beginning of your walkway. You might want to secure it at night with a padlock in order to make it more difficult for a burglar to get away with your television set or stereo.

Hedges are excellent barriers if properly cared for. Of all the barriers available, though, they are the only ones with a monthly maintenance charge. You will want to grow hedges several feet high, and very thick. You don't want a burglar slipping through them. They are certainly not the barrier a chain link fence is, but they can be a nuisance to the burglar—especially if you incorporate some thorned bushes into your total hedge design.

We have some of the simpler things the homeowner can do to keep the burglar away from his property. But if the thief does walk onto your property there are the other deterrents previously discussed.

GOING OUTSIDE OR AWAY

Lawns, Paper and Mail

If the thief sees a lawn that hasn't been cut for a month as well as a few advertising circulars by the front door, will he think the occupants are lazy, or not at home? What would you think? The burglar won't have to think about it long. He will call your phone number, or he will consult the grapevine.

The grapevine for our purposes is made up of your mailman, your paper boy, the man who delivers your dry cleaning, and your beautician, to mention a few. Any time you tell one of them you are leaving your home for any period of time you are courting disaster.

We are not impugning the honesty of your delivery people. In fact, in general they probably classify as the best and most honest people around. So many times, paperboys or delivery men are asked to take money out of their customers' purses and they usually take only what is due to them.

But while your delivery and service people may not steal from you directly they may do so indirectly. If you tell your cleaning delivery man you are leaving town for a few months, he may tell someone else. And a burglar may be around to hear it. Burglars, especially the professionals, have big ears. Eventually they will learn that you have gone on a six month cruise. Bingo. An easy score for the burglar. So instead of cancelling the paper and having the mail held at the post office, especially for shorter trips, ask a close friend or neighbor to pick them up for you. If you are cancelling a service, don't explain why.

More on Delivery People

You may tell the dry cleaning man, who is trusted by you, to drop your clothing off in the bedroom. While there he might see some jewelry which you plan to wear that night, lying on the dresser. Relaxing, after work at a bar, he says, "Gee that

Smith woman has some expensive tastes." The burglar tracks you down.

Bingo, another score for the burglar.

To make the burglar's job more difficult, keep delivery people out of your house. If that is not possible, make sure you don't advertise your wealth to them. While on the subject of advertising, don't keep your valuable china or crystal collection on display in your window. You are inviting the burglar to come to your house.

Another invitation is an open garage door, accompanied by an empty garage. If it is daytime, when most homeowners are likely to be careless, the burglar will slip into the house and quickly remove any portable valuables. Most residence burglaries occur during the daytime—many occurring when the homeowner is away for only 10 or 15 minutes.

Windows

If you don't use them at all, nail them shut. If you do use your windows and are away from home, close and lock them. A burglar's job is too easy as it is.

If you have a window lock, use it. It is useless hanging open. If you want to prevent a burglar from unscrewing the lock by cutting a small hole in your window, you can drip some solder into the screw head.

For cheap security; drill a hole in your window and frame, nail a metal pin into it. It is inexpensive and will baffle the burglar for a while (see chapter two for details). For hard-to-protect casement windows a similar method, with a very short pin which fits tightly into a hole drilled into the latching mechanism, can be utilized.

Doors

If you are in the backyard for a few minutes, or even in the kitchen, lock the front door. Burglars act by stealth. They can slip in and out of your house in a blink of an eye, scooping up an armful of goodies as they leave. A locked front door is the only way to foil the class of burglar known as the "door trier." This burglar tries every door in an apartment building or within an entire neighborhood, looking for the door left open. He will walk into your home and take what he can, quickly. If he runs into you it doesn't worry him. You are the one who will be afraid. He will glibly tell you that he thought this was someone else's house or apartment. And there is little you can do (except lock your door).

Safes and Safe Rooms

Your house should be equipped with a safe room or security room where all the members of your family can go in case an intruder manages to get into your home. We suggest using your bedroom for a security room. Have a phone right by your bed and a lock which you can lock from the inside. A heavy sliding latch will do well. In case you hear an intruder entering your home you can quietly slip the latch, locking your family in the room and the prowler out. The next step is to call the police. You don't want to go out of the room brandishing a baseball bat. The burglar may retaliate with a gun shot.

The door of the security room should be made of good thick hardwood, secure hardware and lock. Windows should have window gates. If your family is safe in this room and a prowler sees no way of getting in he will be frustrated and leave. You should also consider, if you are just starting to build the house, connecting a light switch that will turn on the light in a room at the other side of the house. This will confuse the prowler and perhaps frighten him away. Also, you might want to use special fire-resistant gypsum walling and flooring material, so the room serves the double duty of being able to resist fire.

The security room is a good place to keep your safe. First off, let us say the proper place for most of your valuables is in a safe deposit box. For any valuables you keep at home, though, you should have a safe. Meilink manufactures the Hercules Closet Vault which can be mounted quickly with hammer and screwdriver in a hideway position on your closet shelf. If the vault is in your security room it gives your valuables added protection.

Wall safes require more complicated installation, but are easier to hide. Besides your normal tools a sabre saw would be necessary to make a wall cutout for the vault.

Door Hardware

Are there any exposed screws that the crook can get at quickly? If so you can: (1) remove them; countersink a hole at least 1/4 of an inch into the wood; replace the screws then fill the holes with wood putty; (2) fill the head of the screw with solder or a liquid metal product; (3) use nonretractable screws. Available in many large hardware stores, they are machined so they can be screwed in, but not out. A screwdriver is ineffective because of the special design of the screw. Be sure that any hardware you mount with nonretractable screws is mounted where you really want it. The mounting is permanent.

Sliding Doors

If there is too much play in the sliding door a burglar may be able to lift the door out of its track. Try it yourself. An alert burglar will always check sliding doors. To add protection simply screw a series of metal screws along the upper track of the door to take up any of the play.

A moderately effective locking device for sliding doors—probably better than what you have on your door now—is a narrow piece of wood slipped into the sliding door track. Cut the piece of wood to the proper length (just shorter than the width of the door) and lay it in the track. It is difficult for the burglar to figure out what is holding the door shut and he may get frustrated and leave.

OPERATION IDENTIFICATION

Once the burglar reaches the inside of the house he usually takes his time in deciding what to take. Obviously money and jewelry are his first choices. Next come furs and home entertainment equipment. The burglar can sell all of these items easily to a fence, for a small percentage of their value. But what if the stereo, the television set and other items are marked with the homeowner's name and phone number, or social security number? Would you take these items and risk being caught with merchandise that is so easy to identify?

The solution, then, is to mark your valuables, using a diamond-tipped pen or an engraving tool.

Many police departments will loan you the tools necessary as part of what most communities call Operation Identification. Many police chiefs report drastic reductions in burglaries by using this method. In addition, some provide warning stickers for you to place on doors and windows stating that all property is marked and easily traceable. (Decal courtesy of National Bank of Detroit, "Project Help.")

Some burglars will attempt to alter the numbers with their own diamond tool, so you should probably try to engrave as much information as possible (such as name, phone number and social security number).

Indentifax supplies a kit that includes an engraving tool and a template for scribing the information, as well as warning decals. In addition they provide nationwide registry of your own, specially assigned number, which is listed in a computer bank. If your possessions are stolen in New York and transported to Texas, the police there merely call up the company and ask them to check with the computer for the legal owner of the goods.

As an added protection list the serial numbers of all valuables in your home and store them in your safe deposit box. While you might recognize your television set, unless you can identify it by its serial number it will be difficult for police to prove it was stolen, and for you to get it back.

Burglars and Telephones

Burglars make very good use of the telephone. They call to find out if your house is occupied. If someone answers they will either hang up or say "sorry, wrong number." If you get a rash of either of these type of calls report it to the police and telephone company.

Sometimes burglars who are interested in more detailed information will pose as survey takers. You would be surprised how much people will tell a stranger on the phone if they think it is for a consumer survey. They talk about their personal habits, their earnings, their property holdings, their vacation plans and their sexual preferences. While discussing the last item on the phone may not lead to a burglary, it may lead to a rape.

We suggest that you respect telephone survey takers. They have a job to do. But if they ask any questions that seem irrelevant to you, hang up. There are many more people on the lists of even the legitimate poll-takers. To keep the burglar from using the telephone as a weapon get an unlisted number.

Quickie Security Measures

Keep a list of all emergency phone numbers by each telephone. Don't put your name on your mailbox. The mailman already knows who you are. Even if you live in an apartment house he will list your name by the mailbox. You want the burglar to know as little about you as possible.

Don't advertise travel plans. If you are a member of this nation's higher social strata and feel obligated to have your comings and goings reported on, then tell the local newspapers about your trip after you return.

When you go on a trip tell the police how long you will be gone, how many vehicles will remain in the driveway and whether or not to expect to see lights going on and off during your absence. Give the same information to a close friend and/or neighbor. Ask them to keep an eye on your house. Give one trusted neighbor a key so police can enter your home, if necessary, while you are away.

If you are planning a winter vacation, have your walk and driveway shovelled at every snowfall. And ask a neighbor to put a few footprints in the snow between the driveway and your house. Also ask a neighbor to drive his car up and down your driveway once in a while to leave tracks.

Weddings, funerals and the like are either joyous or sad experiences which are announced in newspapers. You must recognize these occasions as vulnerable times and ask a neighbor to babysit your house.

YOUR BEST DEFENSE

As you can probably tell from some of the suggestions above, neighbors are your best defense. Every block or small community should develop a crime prevention program. It should include education in what is available and necessary for good security (you might want to use this as your textbook) and the establishment of a block-watchers program. Each of your neighbors should assume some of the responsibility for neighborhood protection, looking out for suspicious persons or vehicles in the area. If you see the same car cruising the neighborhood slowly two days in a row, the police should know about it.

You should work together to improve environmental conditions such as street lighting and neighborhood cleanliness. You should meet with the police and tell them what you are doing so they can help.

Don't form a vigilante committee. But you should work together to keep burglars out of your community in a rational manner. Exchange phone numbers with nearby neighbors. If the woman across the street sees a prowler on your grounds she can call you to alert you and then she can call the police.

Remember, your neighbors can be the least expensive and the most effective defense available to you in fighting crime.

section 2 Fire Protection

fire knowledge

Every day more than 2,000 homes burn—more than 700,000 a year. Of the 8,000 people who die in building fires in the United States every year, nine out of ten die at home. Firefighters find their bodies behind a wall of smoke or fire that blocks their escape. Or, too often, they are found where they slept, killed by smoke and toxic gas.

In these blazes property loss exceeds $874 million annually. And statistics gathered by various governmental and consumer protection agencies indicates there is no letup in sight. In fact it is predicted that by 1980 annual property losses from residence fires will total $1 billion or more.

You must attack the fire problem on two fronts, with fire knowledge and with fire equipment (see next chapter).

Home fires take as their victims the very young, and the old and infirm. According to Miklos B. Korodi, manager of residential security systems for ADT, over one third of all those killed by fires are children. At the opposite end of the age spectrum, the over-65 group leads all others in fire-connected fatalities.

The reasoning is simple: "Fire is a merciless killer that takes advantage of physical weakness, inexperience, confusion, and most of all—of those unprepared to react to a sudden conflagration," Korodi says.

Most fires take place between midnight and 6 a.m., when most people are asleep, and conse-quently when there is the greatest danger. And more fires take place in cold than in warm weather. So it is reasonable to assume that fire will strike in the middle of a cold night when you and your family are least able to react to it.

Fire has four distinct stages, starting with the incipient stage and ending in the heat stage. When fire is in its incipient stage, invisible combustion gasses are given off, but there is no smoke, heat, or other sign of danger.

Once a fire smolders and later breaks into flames, it spreads at a catastrophic rate. In many cases people who are sleeping do not awaken in time to escape smoke, noxious gasses, or superheated air, which reach them long before the flames. Fire has been shown to spread so rapidly that from the time flames actually break out a person has, on the average, less than four minutes in which to escape before being overcome by toxic gasses or superheated air.

The only way to prevent tragedy at your house is to develop a sensible fire action plan which includes:

(1) knowing the causes of fire;
(2) eliminating unnecessary fire hazards;
(3) learning how to react to fires; and
(4) using a prepared fire escape plan in case confronted with fire.

To help prevent fires you might want to turn a basement closet into a security closet. You can protect tools you don't want neighbors to borrow or children to play with. At the same time you can store your insecticides and combustible materials. A heat detector will alert you to any fire danger.

Causes of Fire

Preparing food, a simple, everyday process, is one of the major causes of fire in the home. And since food preparation occurs frequently, it is logical to expect the kitchen to be one of the most fire-prone rooms in your house. Grease fires start while food is being fried, and potholders, napkins and curtains often come in contact with flames, all causing fires.

Heating appliances are second on the list of fire hazards. Electric heaters in bedrooms can be dangerous, but even more danger comes from heating plants in the basement where homeowners often store combustible materials. An improperly serviced furnace, for example, may give off sparks or flames which ignite combustible materials.

Cigarette smoking, once the major cause of fire, now rates third. Many people have learned that risking both cancer and a fire from smoking in bed does not make sense. Electricity and appliances in combination are another major cause of fires. Too many appliances on inadequate wiring will cause overheating, which leads to fire. Children playing with matches account for nearly one in ten fires. Flammable fluids are nearly as frequent a fire source. Rags soaked with paint or grease can cause fire simply by spontaneous combustion.

Other causes of residential fire include faulty chimneys and childrens' clothing catching on fire.

Eliminating Fire Hazards

ADT's Korodi recommends that you take a "firewalk" around your home looking for potential fire hazards. His recommendations are incorporated into the following section.

Wiring

With the plethora of appliances available to today's homeowners it is no wonder that circuits become overloaded, wires overheat, and fires start.

According to the Fire Department, the main reason for fires is inadequate or old wiring. With the advent of washing machines, dishwashers and hair dryers, all often being operated on the same circuit at the same time, old wiring will overheat and a fire will start within the wall. Fuses will usually prevent this overheating by "blowing" when too much current is being drawn through the wires. Unfortunately, homeowners often place 20 amp fuses on lines designed to handle only 15 amps. This almost always leads to fire.

Assuming that your house wiring is adequate and that you have not placed the wrong fuse in the circuit, you must still be careful not to overload

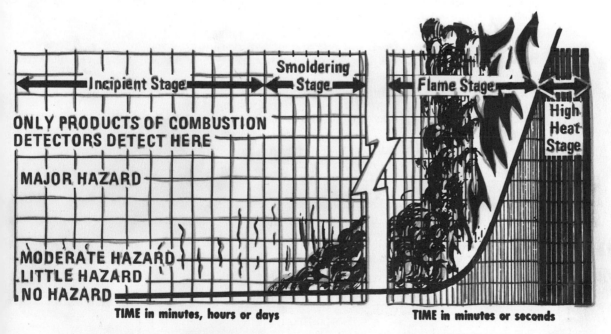

Four stages of fire (Courtesy BRK Electronics).

TEN THINGS YOU SHOULD KNOW ABOUT FIRE HAZARDS*

1. Electric stoves and electrical wiring were the most frequent causes of fire in a recent 12-month period for which statistics were available. They caused nearly 1.3 million fires.

2. Cigarettes, gas stoves, matches, and defective television sets were the next most frequent causes of fire, in that order.

3. There are four distinct phases of fire: (1) the Incipient Stage, when there is no visible smoke or flame; (2) the Smoldering Stage, when there is smoke but no flame; (3) the Flame Stage, when actual fire exists and heat buildup begins, and (4) the Heat Stage, when uncontrolled high heat follows rapidly with an uncontrolled spread of superheated air.

4. While fire is in the Incipient or Smoldering stage it can exist for hours, or even days. Once the Flame and Heat stages are reached, fire can, and usually does, develop with catastrophic speed.

5. Once flames break out a person has, on the average, less than four minutes in which to escape before being overcome by toxic gasses or superheated air.

6. Most fatal home fires occur between midnight and 6 a.m., when family members are asleep.

7. The second floor is the most dangerous floor in the home. Fires on the first floor or in the basement can create gasses that asphyxiate sleepers on the second floor, even if the flames don't reach that level.

8. All burning materials can give off poisonous gasses. Deadly fire-gas fumes result from the burning of wood, nylon, cotton, wool, silk, rayon, furs, paper, rubber, plastic, and leather.

9. Residents should exit immediately from their house when a fire breaks out. They should call the fire department from outside the building, and should never re-enter a burning building.

10. Fire detectors which detect fires before they reach the Flame or Heat stages are more effective than those which react only to high temperatures.

*Information provided by ADEMCO, Alarm Device Manufacturing Company.

extension cords. The Fire Department says that in modern homes extension cords show a dangerous potential for starting fires. If too many appliances are connected on one extension cord the wire will heat up and a fire is likely to start before the fuse blows. You can prevent this by never connecting two heat-producing appliances on the same extension cord. Have a qualified electrician add new wiring where necessary instead of running extension cords throughout your house.

Kitchen fire hazards

Kitchen fires are generally cooking-related. Either the food being cooked catches on fire or combustible materials come in contact with flames or a hot cooking surface. You can prevent this by:

(1) Keeping all cooking surfaces free of grease buildup.
(2) Keeping curtains, napkins, and aprons away from flames.
(3) Keeping all major appliances in good working order by periodic maintenance checkups and immediate service in case of a malfunction.
(4) Keeping appliance cords away from heating surfaces.
(5) Keeping paper bags or newspapers from behind or beside the stove (in case of fire they provide immediate fuel).
(6) Keeping even scorch-resistant potholders away from flame. While they may not scorch they will smolder for hours, resulting in a fire.

Heating-plant fires

Inadequate servicing is the culprit in most gas or oil burner fires.

(1) Burner jets and nozzles should be cleaned.
(2) Flues and chimneys should be inspected for soot buildups which could prevent adequate venting and lead to a fire.
(3) Check electrical space heaters for frayed wires.
(4) Buy only portable space heaters with a tip-over switch; in case you have a space heater sitting on your carpet and it is knocked over there will be no fire danger.

(5) Keep heaters away from drapes and tablecloths. The high temperatures produced by the heater could trigger a fire.

Appliance fires

Incorrect or inadequate wiring within the appliance is the major cause of appliance fires. Korodi recommends all appliances you purchase be certified as safe by Underwriters Laboratory.

Storing combustibles

Nearly everything in your house will burn. But the hazard arises from combustible liquids such as gasoline, solvents and cleaning fluids. You can limit your family's fire hazards by:

(1) limiting the amount of combustible liquids stored in your home;
(2) if you must use them, storing them in your garage in containers approved for that purpose by Underwriters Laboratory;
(3) never allowing old newspapers and rags to accumulate in attics or basements (they provide ready fuel for a hungry fire); and
(4) discarding all oil soaked rags not being used within a few days; spontaneous combustion of oil-soaked rags may be the direct cause of a fire.

Fireplaces

Screen all fireplaces to prevent cinders from escaping. The need for some type of firescreen stems from the danger of flying sparks. There should be no gaps between the edges of the firescreen and the fireplace opening; draw screens rather than standing screens are preferable. When fuel is used which tends to snap, such as cannel coal or some kinds of resinous wood, or when small children are going to be near the fire, the screen should be used continuously. Obviously, a few sparks can get past even the best screen; therefore particularly flammable materials such as paper should not be stored near the hearth.

Never overload a fireplace with paper or wood. The fire may back up, spreading to the rest of the room through sparks or intense heat buildup. And, despite the temptation to let your fire burn out when you go to sleep, don't. An unattended fire can spread easily while you are asleep. Douse the fire with water and make sure the coals are cool.

III. Reacting to Fires

Depending on the location, type and severity of the fire, you will react differently. But here are basic rules.

A. (1) Don't panic.

(2) For most fires you should clear the house of all occupants immediately.

(3) Once you have left the house, call the fire department.

(4) Never return to a burning house—you may be trapped inside.

(5) Don't try to move a blazing pan of grease from the stove. You are likely to spill it, either on the floor or on yourself, spreading the fire.

(6) Don't use water to put out grease fires—it will usually spread it.

(7) Don't use water to put out electrical fires, the shock danger is extremely high.

(8) Don't run if your clothing catches on fire. This fans the flames and spreads the fire. Drop immediately to the floor and roll over again and again until you can be wrapped in a blanket or coat to smother the flames, or are sprayed with water.

Reacting to the aftermath

You should know the basic first aid steps for burns, smoke inhalation and shock.

Burns—small or slight

1. Cool the area with cold water.
2. Apply an antibiotic burn ointment.
3. Wrap with gauze bandage—burned skin is highly susceptible to infection.

Large or serious burns

1. Cool the area with cold water.
2. Remove clothing without tearing the skin.
3. Do not attempt to clean victim and do not use an ointment.
4. Rush to a hospital emergency room.

Smoke inhalation

You should be able to recognize the symptoms, which include unconsciousness or dizziness, irregular breathing, ringing ears, or seeing spots.

1. Lay the victim down in a warm dry place.
2. Give artificial respiration if victim is not breathing.
3. Call fire department for oxygen.
4. Call doctor.

Shock

Shock symptoms include: pale and clammy skin, cold sweats, or irregular breathing.

1. Lay the victim on his back.
2. Elevate legs and hips with blankets or pillows to help blood reach the head.
3. Loosen clothing.
4. Keep the victim warm by wrapping him in a blanket or covering with a coat.
5. Call a doctor.

IV Developing a Fire Escape Plan

The first step in developing your fire escape plan is to control the spread of any fire. The entire family should sleep with bedroom doors shut and the doors to the basement and attic should be kept closed. This prevents the spread of smoke and superheated air for at least a few extra moments.

Conduct another firewalk through your house, or draw your house floor plan on paper, this time selecting primary and secondary escape routes from the bedroom of each member of your family. Choose the windows and doors to be used in case of fire—each should open freely. Instruct family members that if they are ever awakened by the fire alarm they should rush to their doors. If a door is hot to the touch it indicates superheated air in the hallway. They should go instead to a window to escape. If the door is cool it should be opened a little at a time. If flames or superheated air rush in, the door should be slammed and a window used. Arrange a safe rendezvous point—every family member should know where to meet after evacuating the house. This will prevent anyone from making the usually fatal mistake of returning to the house to retrieve a family member who has already escaped to safety.

Practice these routines until they become second nature. In case of a real fire, panic or toxic gasses can cause confusion that will block conscious thought. Unless you know what to do on a subconscious level you may not get out of your house.

Portable ladders

Portable fire escapes are available from a number of manufacturers. The best feature all-steel construction and provide good support and fire resistancy.

We looked at two models from American Lafrance available in our local home improvement center. They come in 15- and 32-foot sizes, costing $16.95 and $29.95 respectively. The length you choose depends on the application.

The fire escape ladders are made of heavy steel link, with steel rungs placed about 18 inches apart, engineered for easy emergency climbing. Two rugged hooks hang over the window sill, helping to keep the ladder away from the burning building. The hooks fold for simple storage of the ladder under a bed or on the floor of a closet.

If you can afford it you should keep one in each bedroom. While two bedrooms may be able to share one ladder, you reduce your family's chance of survival be doing that. Don't count on clear thinking and smokeless hallways during a fire. It may be impossible for your children to reach your bedroom and escape by way of your portable fire escape. Remember, you must have two reasonable avenues of escape in case of fire. We do not consider jumping 15 feet from a second-story window to be a viable alternative. To our way of thinking, a portable fire escape is a necessity.

Have children go through a fire walk at home

fire equipment

Fire alarm systems can be tied into a burglar alarm system, or can operate separately. In any event a fire MUST sound a different alarm than the burglar alarm. You don't want your family hiding from a burglar when they should be running from a fire.

The most widely used sensor in fire alarm systems today is the heat detector. It is a special thermostat that triggers an alarm when the temperature in its vicinity reaches about 135 degrees. We can only recommend these detectors for installation above boilers, ranges and other devices which are likely to cause fires. Used alone they are not much good for your family. By the time the sensor reaches the critical temperature, smoke and gasses may have filled one of the bedrooms. And it is usually the smoke, toxic gasses, or lack of oxygen—not the fire itself—that kills.

One of two systems are recommended in place of this. The smoke detector relies on a photocell which is set to trigger an alarm when the percentage of light passing through a special closed chamber is obscured by a smoke buildup. It gives an earlier warning than the heat detector and can prove to be a vital component in your family fire protection plan. Smoke detectors should be mounted in the hallway outside the bedrooms or in any position which the smoke must pass before reaching the bedrooms.

Another type of fire detector triggers an alarm situation even sooner. It is the products-of-combustion detector also known as an ionization detector. It detects the invisible gasses that are given off by a fire while it is still in its incipient stage. These detectors can provide the extra time your family needs to escape a fire without injury.

BRK Electronics supplies an excellent self-contained unit that installs easily into the ceiling, with screws. It operates on a battery that signals if it is weakening and includes an ear-shattering 110 decibel alarm. The best place to mount the BRK or other products-of-combustion detectors is at the top of any stairwell that leads to a bedroom.

I must say that in home protection, I believe fire detection systems should receive priority over burglar-alarm systems. If you can only afford one type it should be the fire system, although both systems will usually be installed at the same time.

In some localities fire detection systems have become legal requirements for homeowners. Since 1958 Quincy, Massachussetts has required fire detection and alarm devices in all new single-family dwellings. The Village of Bayside, Wisconsin, has a similar ordinance and also requires that occupants perform maintenance checks on the detection systems and report on a standard form to the chief of public safety annually, or be subject to a stiff fine. At the federal level, the Department of Housing and Urban Development requires early-warning fire detectors (smoke or products of combustion) in multiple-family dwellings and in hospitals and nursing homes. Obviously this is an added recommendation for the early-warning type of fire detector.

Extinguishers

Two types can be recommended: (1) The CO_2 fire extinguisher works by smothering the fire—cutting off its oxygen supply; (2) The dry chemical type extinguishes by blanketing the fuel with a powder which turns the heat into an inert gas. Like the CO_2 extinguisher, it works for grease, liquid and electrical fires.

The water-based fire extinguishers, most often seen in office buildings and hotels cannot be recommended for home use. They are too bulky and heavy to be operated easily by all family members. They operate either by a squeeze valve, or by inversion. The standard water fire extinguisher contains 2-1/2 gallons of water (20 pounds) and comes in a heavy metal container. While water fire extinguishers are great for putting out paper fires, they will not handle electrical or flammable liquid fires. Water fire extinguishers are available in the $16 to $20 range.

Several types of dry chemical fire extinguishers are available. Some are designed mostly for electrical and flammable liquid fires while others are designed to handle all fires including wood, paper, upholstery, and similar fires as well as solvent, grease, and appliance fires. Chairs and couches, especially, are often better handled by CO_2 or dry chemical fire extinguishers because many times upholstered furniture has been stuffed with a material that issues a gas when burned. Most CO_2 fire extinguishers handle the same types of fires and need not be considered separately.

These extinguishers can be small, some not much larger than a quart bottle of soda. They range from about 3-1/2 to 8-1/2 pounds and can be operated easily even by children. Generally, compressing a squeeze valve is all that is necessary.

It is essential to keep a fire extinguisher in the kitchen. Grease fires, curtains that catch on fire, or even a fire in your electric range, can be extinguished by the dry chemical extinguisher. If possible keep a fire extinguisher in each bedroom. Or keep a fire extinguisher in a hallway leading to the bedrooms. Keep another fire extinguisher in your workshop or anywhere you store flammable liquids. Prices range upwards of $12.

Mobile homes

Special fire-prevention difficulties exist in mobile homes. Among these are their small size, proximity of heaters and kitchens to sleeping areas, the concentration of combustible materials, lack of adequate escape doors in many cases, and a higher

This heat detector requires no wiring. It is connected to a small radio transmitter that signals a receiver and sounds an alarm when the temperature reaches 135 degrees (Transcience photo).

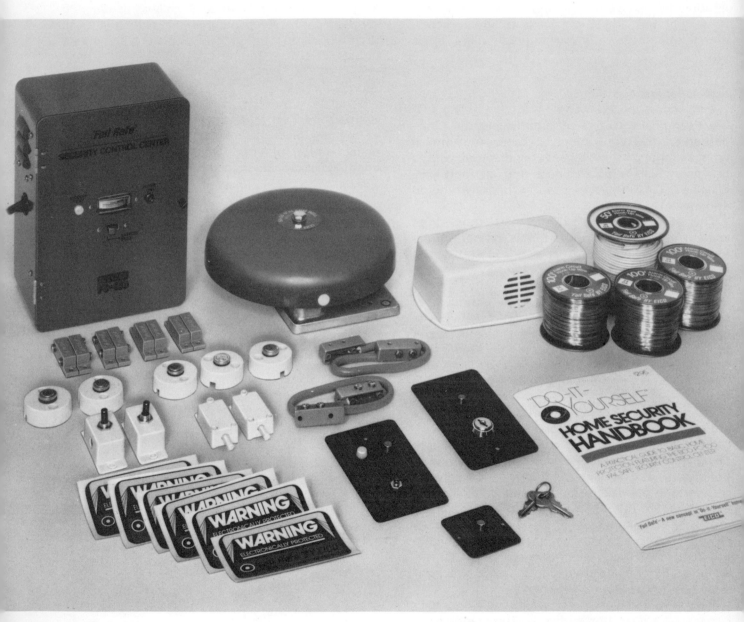

Eico's Burglar-Fire Alarm System uses a key switch mounted by the front door and a loud external bell. Heat detectors are provided for use in kitchens, basements, and boiler rooms. Warning decals can be placed in several locations as a deterrent.

Thermostatic heat detectors, installed in boiler rooms, kitchens, or other rooms where fire is most likely to start, should be mounted on the ceiling to give accurate response to heat. (Westinghouse photo).

Various accessories are available for Eico's home protection system. They can detect: (a) smoke or power failure, (b) freezing temperatures, or (c) moisture or floods.

Early-warning fire detectors should be installed high on a wall or ceiling in the hallway leading to your family's bedrooms (Westinghouse photo).

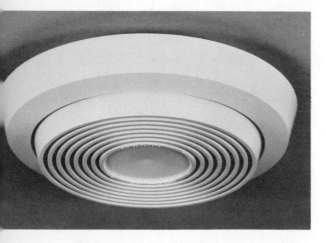

Fires can be detected long before they become dangerous with this self-contained early-warning fire detector from BRK Electronics. The device detects the early products of combustion and sounds a loud horn to warn your family.

An attractively styled early warning fire detector "sniffs" out harmful gasses in the early stages of a fire. The unit from Delta Products plugs into any AC outlet.

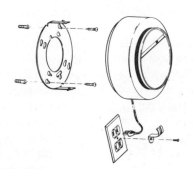

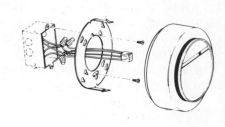

Homeowners have their choice of built-in or plug-in smoke detectors marketed by Westinghouse Security Systems. The unit senses smoke and sounds a built-in alarm to alert occupants.

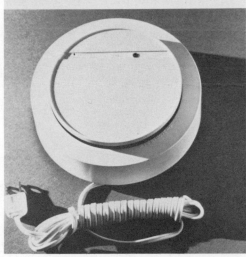

Today's smoke detectors are attractive and easy to install. This unit from Westinghouse is being installed in the best location—the common hallway between the sleeping areas of the house and the kitchen and living room areas.

combustibility of interior finishes than in most site-built homes.

It is estimated that more than 8 million Americans live in mobile homes, with more than 500,000 new units being built annually. While the incidence of fire in mobile homes is about the same or less than in standard homes, data indicate the results are often more serious when a fire occurs.

One study found that the ratio of fatalities in fires in mobile homes was 2.74 times greater than in standard dwellings and that fire losses in a mobile home were 60 percent greater than in a standard home.

In mobile homes, then, it is clear that an early-warning fire detector such as the smoke detector, or preferably the combustion detector, is essential. Of course a small fire extinguisher should be kept close at hand to control fires set in the waking hours.

Sprinklers

Automatic fire extinguishing systems, or sprinklers as they are commonly called, are thought of as protection for commercial establishments or highrise buildings because they are unsightly and expensive. Fortunately, available technology can produce sprinkler systems within the economic reach of many homeowners and attractive enough for home installation. In order for sprinklers to be feasible, however, it is necessary that you have them installed early in the building stages so that pipes can be concealed.

If you can afford the expense of an automatic sprinkler system, it is a wise investment. Sprinklers offer a degree of protection not available from other devices, whether heat detectors or fire extinguishers. Sprinklers can be attached to heat detectors so that they will extinguish fires even while the occupants are not at home and will prevent fire, smoke, and heat-related damage.

Protecting Valuables

Valuables can be lost to fires as well as to burglars—especially if you consider that many times items considered valuable are actually papers such as birth certificates, passports, insurance policies, stock certificates, and deeds.

The best place for these valuables is in your bank in a safe deposit box. But if for one reason or another you do have valuables at home they must be protected from the ravages of fire in a safe rather than in a normal metal file box. And of course, a home safe provides convenience that could not be found in a safe deposit box. Some items that you do not consider important enough to clutter your safe deposit box are important enough to be protected from fire. Many papers, for example, are necessary to keep at home so that you can refer to them. This added convenience alone is worth the cost of installing a safe. If you are a businessman you may take home one-of-a-kind papers from the office to work on at home. And jewelry which you may normally keep in your safe deposit box needs safe storage while at home.

Most heavy-duty safes will keep out the amateur burglar. They can be installed in any room of the house. You might, for example, consider a floor safe for your basement. Or in the basement you might want to have your safe imbedded into a concrete floor. In case you do have priceless jewelry, you do not want a professional team of burglars carrying off the safe. Or you might want to put the safe in your bedroom, using a Hercules wall safe made by the Meilink Steel Safe Company. For added aesthetic value you might choose the Sentry line of safes from John D. Brush Company.

Sentry home safe is concealed in attractive night stand.

Attractive, reasonably priced Survivor is part of the Sentry line of fire-resistant safes and files. Its low price makes it feasible for many homeowners to have their own home safe deposit box.

This Sentry Survivor was in an intense fire which gutted an entire home. Special design prevented the papers inside from charring even though temperatures in the fire probably exceeded 2,000 degrees.

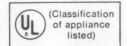

Papers and jewelry can be protected from the ravages of fire in this Meilink Hercules vault. Its double steel walls are insulated to withstand temperatures up to 1,700 degrees, for a period of one hour.

These safes are made to look like attractive bedside tables.

In any event you will want to invest in a good fireproof safe—a safe that not only does not burn, but keeps the documents inside from charring or burning. In intense home fires, temperatures may reach over two thousand degrees. In a home fire a normal steel box used by most homeowners would be cremated in five minutes or less. Even a steel safe may not prevent documents from charring if subjected to this temperature for more than a few minutes. Many fireproof safes are insulated with a material that contains free-floating or latent moisture. When subjected to the heat of an intense fire the moisture forms steam vapors, keeping the paper inside from charring. The principle is simple—steam forms at 212 degrees, and paper does not begin to char until it reaches a temperature of 340 degrees. As long as the steam is present it serves as a heat barrier.

Check any safe you buy for Underwriter's Laboratories labels. This means that UL has put the safe through extensive testing, which may include an hour in a furnace reaching temperatures of 1700 degrees or more plus a thirty-foot drop onto concrete while the safe is still red-hot. This can be compared to the safe in your bedroom dropping directly to the basement, once the floor is burned away during a fire. Some companies do not attempt to get UL certification although they put their safes through similar tests. The Listing Mark generally appears in one of the forms shown above left, together with the product designation.

section 3 Preventive Medicine

building with security in mind
fire and burglary

All of the burglary and fire prevention methods discussed in this book can best be implemented while you are still in the early stages of building your home or of having it built, although you can order the best of the locks we have recommended on the best doors possible at any time. But if you are still in the planning stages of home designing you can accomplish much more.

Many architects and urban planners agree that the effective design of residential environments can create the feeling of physical security, which in itself inhibits crime. This includes not only where on your lot you locate your home but also where your home is in comparison to others on your block.

DEFENSIBLE SPACE

This theory, first thought to be applicable only to the design of apartment houses, can also work for the builder/developer who is planning a large development of one-family dwellings.

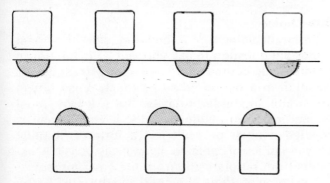

Shaded areas represent effective defensible space. In left diagram, homeowners do not feel much responsibility for cars or people passing by because they may be going on to the next block, or through to

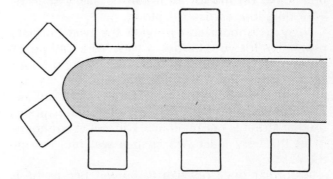

the other side of town. In right diagram, street dead ends. Each homeowner feels responsible for the actions that take place on his block. Defensible space extends through the entire area.

Oscar Newman first coined the term "defensible space" for his theory of how architecture can affect crime. He came up with this basic definition: "Defensible space is a surrogate term for the range of mechanisms—real and symbolic barriers, strongly defined areas of influence and improved opportunities for surveillance—that combine to bring an environment under the control of its residents."

With Newman's theory as a guide, we discover that placing a home back far from the street on a large lot, or building a house that seems to be its own environment, rather than flowing into the environment around it, can be a genuine cause of increased crime.

The idea of defensible space is to have a house extend its territoriality—that feeling of belonging to the area around it—and to make the residents feel that their lot and even a part of the street outside, are part of their own, personal space.

The territoriality or personal space feeling can be created by locating the house close to the street, or at least towards the front portion of the lot. A stoop or step should lead up to the house. This should be connected to the sidewalk by a well-defined walkway. Thus the house extends itself onto the stoop and the stoop, onto the street.

Also part of the personal space concept is the architect's allowance for natural surveillance of the street. Windows should be so placed that occupants can easily observe the comings and goings of people on the street. And your house should be positioned on the lot so it can be easily seen by your neighbor across the street.

Nosy neighbors can provide the best burglary protection for you. In fact, a New York City police captain explained that in the older neighborhoods of the city, "the little old lady who sits by her window all day is the best deterrent to crime." The woman, who feels that anything that happens on that street is her business, will yell at strangers, or at the very least will keep a watchful eye on them.

A burglar does not like to be watched as he is casing your house because it could lead to his apprehension later. So if a few neighbors like to sit in the windows and talk about what they see,

they should. And if your house is visible to them, they will serve as guards for it.

This reasoning helps explain the defensible space theory. To the woman in the window, anything that goes on in the street beneath her is within her sphere of influence. A feeling of an increased sphere of influence can be purposely created by a building developer. Instead of designing streets so they run parallel or perpendicular to each other, the builder should incorporate into his design streets that dead-end.

Looking at the diagram you can see that any neighbor could consider the entire dead-end street within his domain. If a car drives into that street the driver had better pull into a spot in front of one of the houses and visit a fellow homeowner. If not, then he must be a potential burglar. In a small dead-end arrangement like this, neighbors begin to feel more neighborly. They will walk outside and ask the driver of an unfamiliar car if they can help him. This irks the burglar and may make him steer clear of the neighborhood.

With defensible space in mind and with this book close at hand, it is a good idea to sit down with a builder and an architect and discuss the security design of your new home. And a builder planning a number of houses in a new development might well consider conferring with a security consultant. While it is still true that picture-pretty kitchens sell new homes, you will find that built-in burglar alarms, fire alarms, or perhaps even a fenced community, are what today's homeowners are looking for.

Site Choice

When deciding on a building site, the most important question to ask yourself is: is the house isolated? Of course there are many reasons for isolation in a period when so much noise rattles our brains in the large cities. But a lesson must be learned from medieval days: If your house is isolated it must be built like a fortress. It must be self-sufficient, able to handle all possible assaults from burglars and from the environment.

The home of Roman Polanski and the late Sharon Tate was isolated by most city or suburban living standards, but certainly nowhere as isolated as the vacation home you may be planning. Yet, because of the isolation no one was aware of the grisly murders that took place there, until the next morning. And the isolation in this instance was only a matter of several hundred yards. We are not trying to scare you with stories of the Bogeyman stalking the woods. But we do want to drive home the point that if your home is isolated it must have added protection.

Let's look at a couple of things we would recommend to help protect your vacation home, and then, if your home is at all isolated you might want to implement some or all of these procedures.

The Isolated Home

If you are having a cabin or vacation home built for you you should consider some of the following features:

CENTRAL STATION ALARM—running a leased telephone line from your mountain hideaway to the nearest town can be very expensive. An alternative could be an alarm with an automatic dialer which will summon police if an alarm condition exists.

Ask phone and power companies if they will consider burying their lines. This should present no problem in ecology-conscious America, and will prevent the burglar from cutting off your power supply, and your link with the outside world.

POWER SUPPLY—consider installing an emergency generator, strictly for power backup in case of flooding or other environmental disasters. From a burglary prevention standpoint this is crucial also. Without lighting you could be at a burglar's mercy. Without any power at all, at nature's mercy. In any event a power supply is a good idea. Second choice is an emergency lighting system that will switch itself on in case of power failure.

GOOD LOCKING HARDWARE—you want the best lock you can get for your vacation hideaway. Doors should be protected with the Fichet Vertibar lock, one of the toughest to pick or force. Windows should have strong, key-operated locks.

POLICE PROTECTION—let the police know how long you will be away from the vacation home and ask them to check on it for you periodically.

In turning your vacation home into a fortress you might find that it is not at all difficult and that the same procedures can, and should, be applied to your year-round home.

Barriers

There are six very different types of barriers that you can use to protect your home:

(1) natural barriers—mountains and moats;
(2) structural barriers—fences;
(3) mechanical barriers—locks;
(4) energy barriers—alarms, lights, bells;
(5) human barriers—guards;
(6) animal barriers—dogs.

While in the building or planning stages of construction you will want to take advantage of as many of these barriers as possible. In site selection you might consider a home with a mountain or a canyon behind it to be your best bet. It's not only beautiful, it gives great protection to one side of your home.

Landscaping

This can be one of the most important aspects in planning security into your home. Keep it simple. Remember that small plants may one day grow into a jungle. The small apple tree you plant near your home may become a stairway to the second story windows.

Before you do any landscaping you might want to think about your total security package, considering all aspects of security discussed in this book. Consider placement of inside and outside lights, location of windows and doors, laying electrical lines underground to protect them from burglars, etc.

For example, you will want some floodlights or mercury vapor lamps on a post up to 50 feet away from your home. Before landscaping is done, that site should be selected and conduit should be run. You will find that at this point in home building these lights can be easily wired to a switch in the master bedroom.

The same builders that take exquisite care in selecting the most durable and practical materials for your home generally skimp on its security.

Doors and Windows

We have mentioned this before but it is worth mentioning again. Doors are weak links in your home's perimeter because they are frequently poorly constructed or positioned. Openings for doors are generally built too large, so the door and jamb can fit easily in the space provided. Wedges of wood are forced between the jamb and the opening in an attempt to secure the door in the correct position. But this method merely holds the door in place, waiting to be attacked by a door forcer or frame bender.

If the distance between the jamb and opening is slight, there is little to gripe about. But if it isn't you should use long strips of plywood rather than a few wedges, to fill the entire space. In addition, extra bracing wood can be used around the door opening. Doors should be at least 1 3/4 inches hardwood, with two inches preferred. Panels should be avoided. If you do not like the look of a flush door you can add on molding to form panels of your own design.

The number of doors should be limited. No matter how large the house, you need no more than three doors. Work with your architect to come up with the correct placement of doors to allow your family free access to the house, while limiting the burglar's access.

Sliding glass doors continue to be popular. They can be included in your house design, but special care must be taken in protecting them. Inspect the door to see if it can be lifted from its track. If it can, insert metal screws into the top channel, closing the gap.

Excessive use of windows can be argued against on several grounds. They waste energy by increasing both heating and air-conditioning costs and prove to be another weak link in the home security chain. Reinforce the chain by incorporating decorative metalwork into home design. Ornamental grills, whether purchased at a home supply store or custom designed, can serve as a special accent for your windows and provide extra protection. Consider using burglar-resistant glass for large picture windows or for glass windows in doors. Chances are that you will not want to put a large grill on a picture window. And without it the only

way to keep a burglar out is to have burglar-resistant glass installed during construction.

Locks

A dual emphasis on security and styling in locking hardware has turned the plain, unadorned lock into a thing of the past. Now you can get locks and associated hardware in a variety of designs, ranging from ornate French and Italian designs to strikingly contemporary models. Lock manufacturers have made significant strides in reconciling security and high style. Today's locking hardware is designed to be compatible with as many door styles as possible, while, at the same time offering a heavy-duty locking mechanism.

We have mentioned the desirability of having a one-inch deadbolt. Many builders are familiar with this term because it has been written into many building codes. As this becomes more widespread, home handymen, as well as builders, should be prepared to put a one-inch deadbolt on every entrance door.

More and more one-inch deadbolts are showing up with steel roller bars inside that make it virtually impossible to saw through the lock. Latches are also increasing security. While the standard latch used to be 3/8 of an inch, the standard has been moved to 1/2 inch, providing extra protection against forced entry.

Our recommendation for each door is a high quality mortise lock or a Schlage Series G with a one-inch bolt. If you have decided on a door that has any glass panels, be sure to install a double-cylindered lock. And all sliding doors should have Adams Rite locks which give protection comparable to an adequate front door lock.

Fireplace Facings and Hearths

There are fireplace facing safety standards for combustible materials such as wood trim or paneling. There should be 3 1/2 inches minimum clearance on all sides of the fireplace opening. If the wood projects more than 1 1/2 inches at the top of the opening, then the minimum clearance would be 12 inches at that point.

The front fireplace hearth should extend 8 inches on each side of the fireplace opening and 16 inches out in front for minimum safety requirements. For both the hearth and the facing you should consult local codes, since requirements vary across the country.

Alarms

You can save more than $100 by installing the alarm during construction. One of the major costs of post-construction alarm installation is concealing wires behind the walls (done for security as well as aesthetics). You can avoid this cost by planning in advance.

While your house is in the early-construction stages you can call an alarm installer who will plan the routes for most of the wires, drill holes for some of the sensors, and make a rough cut for the alarm control box. There are many added features (such as additional panic buttons and sensors) that you will be able to buy with the money saved by having an alarm installation begun at this time. Even if you are a do-it-yourselfer you can still realize big savings by installing the alarm early.

If you are planning a pool, you might consider running alarm wire out to it and rigging up a moisture detector which will alert you if anyone falls into your pool.

Planning a large vegetable garden? Run a set of wires out to the site of your family's future farm. Later, connect a frost detector which will warn you when young plants are in danger.

BUILDERS BEWARE!

Building sites are more vulnerable to burglary than are completed homes. The construction industry loses upwards of $500 million annually to construction site thefts.

The reason? Builders do not consider unfinished homes to be targets. Yet wood, copper pipes, bricks, appliances and tools are ripped off from individual and large-development sites daily.

Protecting the Site

Security procedures can be as simple as putting up a fence, or as complex as installing a radar-type alarm to protect a large construction site. One builder spends less than $10 a month on yellow paint, dipping the bottom half of his metal stakes into the paint so they are easily identifiable. He estimates he saves $900 a month.

The choice of protection methods must be determined by the value of the goods to be protected. Follow this rule: Don't try to protect $1,000 worth of building materials with a $10 security system. Conversely: don't try to protect $10 worth of building materials with a $1,000 system.

To spend the least amount possible on site protection you should spend the money on the perimeter of the site. While use of armed guards and dogs does work for builders, a fence is a good protective device, serving as a psychological as well as a physical barrier. After construction it can be used on another site. Builders agree that an eight-foot chain link fence with a 45 degree barbed wire top provides adequate protection.

For the person building his own home, installing a temporary chain link fence can be costly, so it might be a good idea to use an alternative method such as installing your burglary lights in the early stages of construction. Lighting is a cheap but good deterrent. Along with the lights, post signs warning that the area is patrolled by a guard force. The criminal is likely to believe this to be true, thinking there would be no reason to have lights on unless someone might be patrolling the grounds.

Construction Trailers

Statistics show that more than half of all on-site burglaries occur in the trailers. The most valuable tools and supplies are stored in trailers, yet trailers are usually provided with the least adequate methods of protection.

Use padlocks on the trailer and leave them closed when not in use. If you leave a padlock hanging open all day, a burglar will make note of the type of padlock you are using, purchase a similar model, and replace your padlock with his. At night he returns and uses his own key or combination to open the lock and get at your tools.

Protect the trailer windows with metal gates, or at least with chicken wire. Use a small, inexpensive alarm on doors and windows. If you are planning on building more than one house, you might want to have guards patrolling your construction sites.

Selling Security

Thirty-two construction industry executives participating in a recent survey predicted that in the period 1975 to 1980 one in ten homes will be built with a security system, and walled cities will be considered. And housing developers are now finding that they must seriously consider security systems in all new developments.

There are several aspects to this concern. First, builders must measure the willingness of renters or buyers to pay a premium to deflect the cost of built-in security amenities. A recent sampling of builder experience indicates that these costs can be covered, especially if the per-unit cost is kept low by requiring acceptance of the security system in all units, and if the security system fits easily into the total sales package.

A second aspect of builder concern is the effect security, or the lack of it, has on sales. Some builders who offer residential unit security as part of their package are claiming that security has noticeably increased their sales. A further concern is the legal aspect of security. Minimum security standards are being considered in several parts of the country. Before long, minimum security standards could be required for multi-unit dwellings.

These three points, as well as the astonishing rise in property crime, should be considered when making a decision about building security into a new home.

termite protection

Termites are estimated to cause close to $350 million worth of damage every year, even though termite infestation can be recognized and caught at an early enough stage to prevent serious damage.

The first place to check for termite damage should be any earth-filled area covered by concrete, such as steps, the porches, or a landscape planter. From these areas, where the termites have their subterranean nests, termites can spread out to nearby wood. They then crawl upward through openings in slab or foundation walls; a crack as thin as a sheet of paper can admit termites. To cross exposed areas they construct mud tunnels which are easily identifiable, usually spanning wood joists or sills. Look throughout the entire perimeter of your house for these tunnels, and subsequent decay.

This type of examination is usually best carried out from below. Probe exposed wood parts with your screwdriver. If the point penetrates more than is normal, this may indicate termites. Where possible, remove any wood in contact with the ground, since this provides termites with ideal access.

GEOGRAPHICAL AREAS NEEDING PROTECTION

Although it is possible for termites to be found all over the United States (with the exception of Alaska), the infestation rate in Maine, Vermont, New Hampshire, Minnesota, and the Dakotas is extremely low; damage in these areas is not probable. For the most part, termites are found wherever the mean average temperature exceeds 45 degrees. The farther south you go, the more prevalent they are.

PROTECTIVE MEASURES

Control measures for termite infestation include:

(1) adequate drainage for the site and building;
(2) adequate clearance between ground surfaces and lumber;
(3) adequate ventilation of structural spaces;
(4) proper flashing;
(5) and the removal of all stumps, roots, fallen timber, or other wood debris.

CORRECTIVE MEASURES

Certain types of construction are particularly susceptible to termite infestation, due to unprotectable wood near the ground. In these cases, a chemical barrier is needed.

CONCRETE SLAB ON-GROUND CONSTRUC-

TION—soil treatment or treated wood is recommended.

MULTIPLE LEVEL CONSTRUCTION—such as split-level designs, may require soil treatment protection to avoid hidden access of termites.

CONSTRUCTION DETAILS AT ENTRANCE PLATFORMS—also porch slabs, planter boxes, partially veneered sections, etc., will probably require soil poison as supplement to physical barriers.

As is true with so many protection procedures, termite control is easiest *before* a house is built. Most good builders in heavy termite regions will pretreat site, but you should always ask before buying or building a new house.

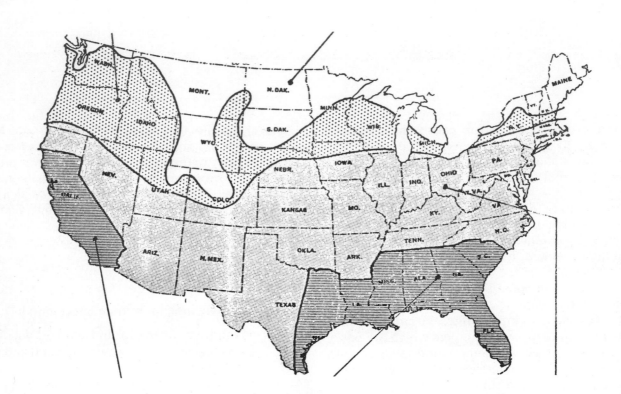

TERMITE SUSCEPTIBILITY BY GEOGRAPHIC AREA

a. Region I (including Hawaii): termite protection required in all areas.

b. Region II: termite protection generally required, although specific areas are sometimes exempted.

c. Region III: termite protection usually not required, except specific local areas that have been found hazardous.

d. Region IV (including Alaska): termite protection not required.

SOURCE: U.S. Department of Housing and Urban Development (HUD) *Minimum Property Standards*. Washington, D.C.: Government Printing Office.

lightning protection

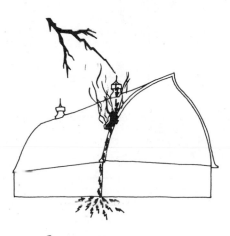

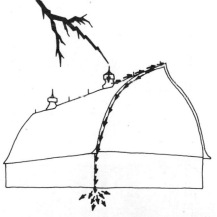

On unprotected buildings (top), a lightning bolt may follow any path of low resistance—usually metal—to the ground, and can cause damage anywhere along that path. On protected buildings (bottom), the lightning conductors provide a direct path to the ground (from Farmers' Bulletin no. 2136, Washington D.C.: Government Printing Office).

Lightning—a discharge of pent-up electricity—travels in a zigzag, jagged pattern and searches out the strongest electric-field line between the cloud that produced it, and the ground or another cloud. A recent two-year study of lightning casualties by the Lightning Protection Institute indicates some startling conclusions as to the relative dangers of lightning according to location. Homes were the number one lightning casualty site, with 26.8 percent of the casualties. Other categories and figures were: open ground, 23.2 percent; under a tree, 13.6 percent; water or beach, 11.4 percent; farm, industrial, or institutional buildings, 10.8 percent; open vehicles, 10.0 percent; a camp or summer cottage, 4.2 percent.

LIGHTNING IN THE HOME

Lightning can enter a building in four ways:

(1) as a direct strike on the building (although lightning very rarely strikes sides of buildings);
(2) after striking a metal object (such as a television antenna or track extending out from the building), and then coursing down the metal attachments on the house;

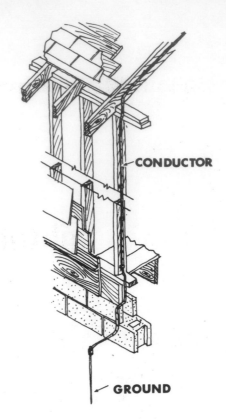

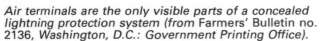

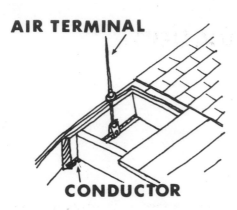

Air terminals are the only visible parts of a concealed lightning protection system (from Farmers' Bulletin no. 2136, Washington, D.C.: Government Printing Office).

Ground connections are made through the base of the building wall in concealed lightning protection systems (from Farmers' Bulletin no. 2136, Washington, D.C.: Government Printing Office).

Lightning protection points for a house: (1) terminals spaced a minimum of twenty feet apart along ridges and within two feet of ridge ends; (2) downlead conductors; (3) at least two grounds each at least ten feet deep, for the house (additional grounds may be used for clothesline, fence, etc.); (4) roof projections are tied into the conductor system; (5) protection for tree; (6) at least two terminals on chimneys; (7) dormers rodded; (8) arrester on antenna, connected to the main conductor; (9) tie-in to conductor system of gutters within six feet of conductor; (10) arrester on overhead power lines (from Farmers' Bulletin no. 2136, Washington, D.C.: Government Printing Office).

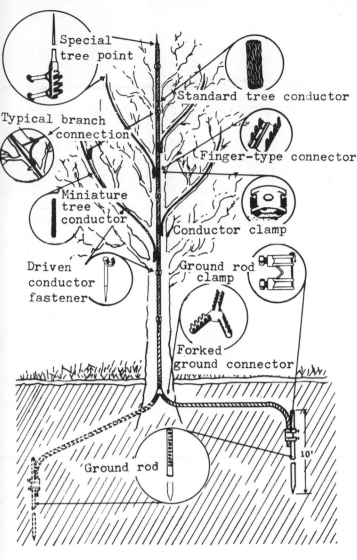

Valuable trees should have lightning protection (from Farmers' Bulletin no. 2136, Washington, D.C.: Government Printing Office).

death as the bolt travels that path. Any point that the bolt is likely to strike or to which the current might sideflash, must be protected. And DON'T make the mistake of thinking that your television antenna gives you lightning protection; it is a lightning target! The average antenna is grounded and equipped with a lightning arrester, but does not offer protection to the house. The grounding is not sufficient, nor are enough paths to earth provided. Often the antenna attracts lightning, and cannot handle the current. The bolts skip over to plumbing and wiring, damaging walls and appliances or causing flash fires.

Adequate lightning protection for a home consists of six areas of protection concentration. Although homes in isolated areas are the most susceptible to lightning strikes, all homes should have these six areas covered.

(1) Air terminals: copper or aluminum terminals, ten inches or higher, should be placed at a maximum of twenty feet apart on the highest points of the roof and all projections; they should be sized, anchored, and spaced according to the National Fire Protection Association's Protection Code and Underwriters Laboratories requirements for Master Label. Chimneys must have separate air terminals.

(2) Main conductors: these are special heavy copper or aluminum cables that interconnect all air terminals on the roof, with at least two conductors to ground.

(3) Branch conductors: lengths of cable similar to that used in main conductors, but smaller, to connect into the main conductor system all plumbing stacks, antennas, gutters, air-conditioning, water pipes, telephone grounds, and other major metal units within six feet of the conductors.

(4) Lightning arresters: small devices which mount at the entrance points of overhead electrical service wires and on the television antenna. They connect to the system's grounding in order to arrest surges of power up to a few hundred amperes, and are primarily for distant lightning strikes.

(3) following a power line or ungrounded wire fence;

(4) striking a nearby tree and leaping over to the building to find a better path to the ground.

Lightning usually follows a metallic path to the ground (and from the ground up). The bolt may leap from this path to wiring or plumbing, causing fires or burning out appliances.

A good lightning protection system should provide an easy, direct path for the bolt to follow to the ground, and must prevent injury, damage, or

(5) Grounding: for small houses on moist clay soil, at least two ground rods will be needed, 1/2 inch in diameter or larger; copper is preferred, put at opposite corners of the house and sunk a minimum of ten feet into the moist earth. For high-resistance sand, gravel, or rocky soil, use special counterpoise or other grounding systems. Larger houses will need more than two grounds.

(6) Tree protection: any tree taller than the house and within ten feet of the house needs a special tree system (discussed further on in this chapter).

GROUND CONNECTIONS

The ground connections installed may determine the efficiency of your entire lightning-protection system. At least two grounds are needed for each system. They should be spaced as far apart as possible—usually at opposite corners of a building—and should reach below and away from the building in order to avoid lightning damage to the walls. Ground connections can be made in four ways: (1) by clamping the conductor cable to a copper-clad or galvanized-steel rod which has been driven at least ten feet into the ground; (2) by stranding copper conducting cable and burying it in a trench; (3) by clamping copper conducting cable to a sheet metal plate that has been buried; (4) by clamping the conductor to a metal water pipe.

The major factor involved is a good, permanent connection between the lightning protection system and moist earth. Putting a short length of a conductor cable into the earth is not enough; it does not give sufficient electrical contact.

An important point to remember is that the soil in which the ground is to be made could damage ground connections. Certain soil or chemical substances may corrode ground connections. Heavily galvanized steel resists corrosion for long periods in any soil; copper and copper-clad steel resist corrosion indefinitely in soil if it is relatively free of ammonia. Aluminum corrodes in soil and should never be used for ground connections.

PROTECTING EXISTING STRUCTURES

If you are adding a lightning-protection system to an already-constructed house, a "semi-concealed" system may be best. Such a system includes the parts previously listed, and may use the same types of air terminals as a built-in system. Conductors are installed by placing them behind downspouts and other building features. Weather-resistant materials are used, and special fasteners are included for attachment to specific materials—wood, masonry, or stone. The ground rod connections are made by running conductors into the soil alongside the wall, and then underground for several feet (at least two) to the rods.

BUILDING IN LIGHTNING PROTECTION

There are several advantages to putting lightning protection in while the building is being erected. Protection is effective immediately; parts are protected and concealed, and installation costs may be lower.

The old three-to-five foot lightning rods have been replaced by air terminals which may be as short as ten inches; copper air terminals are the least conspicuous. They are usually slender and can be neutral in color, or you may select a particular architectural design to enhance barren roof areas.

For detailed information on installation for specific types of buildings and homes, or for farm, industrial, and commercial uses, write to Lightning Protection Institute, 2 North Riverside Plaza, Chicago, Illinois 60606 (no charge for information).

TREE PROTECTION

Tens of thousands of trees in backyards, parks, boulevards, and pastures are destroyed by lightning every year. There has, however, been increasing use of special copper lightning protection systems to preserve shade trees. Reasons for their use are many. To name the most obvious: the copper lightning protection systems provide greater safety for people seeking shelter from the rain; they cut down on the cost of removing lightning-killed trees, and of buying new trees; they give protection to nearby buildings; and, in farm areas, they offer greater protection to livestock huddled beneath during a storm.

Special lightning protection equipment for trees is available. Copper is recommended; substitutes may corrode. Copper systems also look better because they discolor to a shade that resembles bark, and they do not harm the tree.

A main terminal point is placed as high up as it can be securely fastened, and miniature terminal points are clamped onto main branches. The main conductor is a 32-strand, 17-gauge copper cable that runs from the main terminal to a 14-strand, 17-gauge copper cable which attaches to the branch terminals. Grounds are usually two or more 1/2-inch to 3/4-inch rods driven to a ten-foot depth away from the main root system. Special soil conditions may require special grounding. Trees with trunks more than three feet in diameter need two down-conductors on opposite sides of the trunk. The cables are attached to the tree with fasteners that hold them away from the trunk. These attachments are spaced three to four feet apart.

If the grounding of a building is within twenty-five feet of a protected tree, the two systems may be interconnected. Or if there are several large trees in a row, a common grounding may be used as long as depth grounds are no more than eighty feet apart.

MAINTENANCE

Lightning-protection systems should be inspected every year. Look for bent, loose, or missing air terminals; for broken conductor cables, and for loose connecting clamps. Lightning arresters should be checked periodically to determine the possibility of leakage of electrical energy. This check should be made by someone familiar with the equipment and electric current measurements.

PERSONAL SAFETY

Because more people are injured in unprotected homes than in any other location, you should follow these rules if caught in an unprotected home during a lightning storm. Stay away from metal objects such as prefabricated fireplaces, stoves, water faucets, appliances, telephones, and metal windows. Stay inside! If caught outside, lie down in a depressed spot, or under a ledge or rock overhang. Stay away from tall or isolated trees.

wind protection

If your home is located in a high-wind area, you should be concerned about broken glass, shingles blowing off, structural damage, and falling trees. The risk of wind damage can be assessed by checking with your local weather bureau, or looking at the accompanying wind map. Even checking the weather bureau may not tell you what you need to know; weather department records really cover only the winds at the station. You are concerned with the conditions around your home, which may be several miles away. So the "microclimate" caused by geographic features is important. If you are building or buying talk to neighbors and examine the area to see if many trees have been blown down in earlier windstorms.

GLASS

There are definite standards set by building codes on the strength of glass to be used in high wind areas. Double strength glass, tempered glass, or plate glass is specified in certain areas depending on the size of the window and the wind velocity. Before building or remodeling, check with your local building code or with the nearest office of HUD (Department of Housing and Urban Development) for requirements. Of course, all storm doors should be glazed with tempered glass or acrylic plastic.

SHINGLE SAFETY

The best guarantee for shingle security is adequate nailing or adhesive. Because of their good resistance to wind, many home builders choose a self-sealing strip asphalt shingle. This is a shingle in which short strips or spots of factory-applied adhesive are positioned in a row to meet the underside of the shingle tabs of the strip above. The shingle weight, with the softening adhesive under the sun, makes a firm connection to keep the shingle tabs from blowing up during periods of high winds. These shingles are particularly desirable on lower pitched roofs.

On existing roofs, where the shingles were not of the seal-down type, a small dab of roofing cement applied with a putty knife under each tab will provide the same security as factory-made seal-down shingles.

The amount of shingle measuring from the bottom of its butt edge upslope to the next overlapping butt edge is called "shingle exposure". This distance should not exceed that specified by the manufacturer. Follow manufacturer instructions on

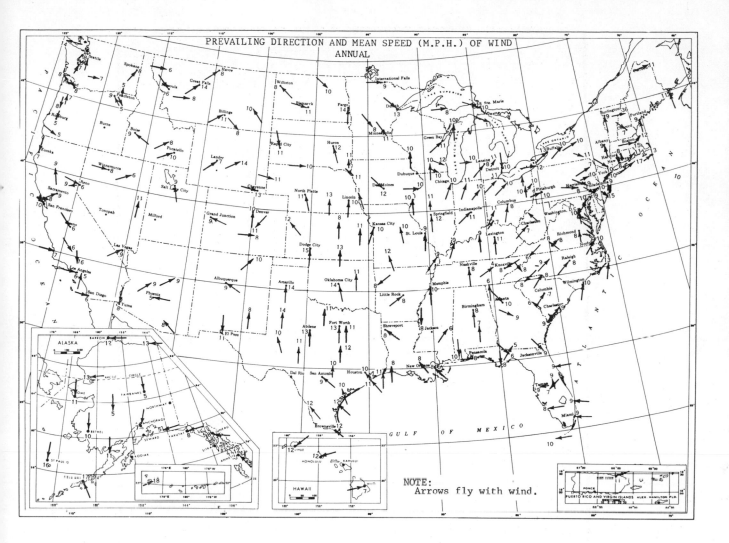

exposure so that seal-tab strips occur at the proper points.

Shingle Selection

Asphalt shingles are available in a wide range of weights, colors and patterns. Shingle lines vary from one manufacturer to another. However, the great bulk of shingles sold are of the strip type, approximately 12 inches wide by 36 inches long with three foot-wide shingle tabs which are separated by real slots or embossed slot simulations. The strip shingles are usually designed for 5 inch exposure and a 2 inch headlap meaning that at any given point in the roof surfacing, there are at least two shingle thicknesses.

Choice in design and appearance of strip shingles has broadened in recent years. Color variations and color blends have expanded. Double-layering and extra felt weights have brought thicker shingle butts. Irregular cutting of the butts has given some shingle designs a random appearance which lends texture to the roofing surface.

Size and number of nails per shingle strip are usually specified in instructions included with the shingles or on the carton. Usually this is one nail on each end and one above each slot. In highwind areas the Housing and Urban Development Department's Minimum Property Standards specificies six nails per strip. Nails should be galvanized, large head roofing nails, at least 3/4 inches long. When using self-sealing strip shingles, be sure your nailing avoids going into the adhesive strips or above the line of them.

Insurance

Most homeowner policies cover wind damage, but be sure to specify such coverage when arranging an insurance policy. Putting off repairing loose

TOTAL NUMBER OF TROPICAL CYCLONES, LOSS OF LIFE AND DAMAGE							
	Total Number Tropical Cyclones*		Total Number Hurricanes		Loss of Life		Damage by Categories**	
Year	All Areas	Reaching U.S. Coast	All Areas	Reaching U.S. Coast	Total All Areas	United States	Total All Areas	United States
1942	10	3	4	2	17	8	7	7
1943	10	4	5	1	19	16	7	7
1944	11	4	7	3	1,076	64	8	8
1945	11	5	5	3	29	7	8	8
1946	6	4	3	1	5	0	7	7
	48	20	24	10				
1947	9	7	5	3	72	53	8	8
1948	9	4	6	3	24	3	7	7
1949	13	3	7	2	4	4	8	'3
1950	13	4	11	3	27	19	7	7
1951	10	1	8	0	244	0	7	6
	54	19	37	11				
1952	7	2	6	1	16	3	6	6
1953	14	6	6	2	3	2	7	7
1954	11	4	8	3	720+	193	9	9
1955	12	5	9	3	1,518+	218	9	9
1956	8	2	4	1	76	21	8	7
	52	19	33	10				
1957	8	5	3	1	475	395	8	8
1958	10	1	7	0	49	2	7	7
1959	11	7	7	3	57	24	7	7
1960	7	5	4	2	185	65	8	?
1961	11	3	8	2	345	46	8	6
	47	21	29	8				
1962	5	1	3	0	4	4	6	6
1963	9	1	7	1	7,218+	11	9	7
1964	12	6	6	4	266	49	9	9
1965	6	2	4	1	76	75	9	9
1966	11	2	7	2	1,040	54	8	7
	43	12	27	8				
1967	8	2	6	2	68	18	8	8
1968	7	3	4	2	11	9	7	7
1969	13	3	10	2	364	256	9	9
1970	7	4	3	1	74	11	9	8
1971	12	5	5	3	44	8	8	8
	47	17	28	10				
Total	291	108	178	57				
Mean	9.7	3.6	5.9	1.9				

**The Environmental Data Service has for some time recognized that, without detailed expert appraisal of damage, all figures published are merely approximations. Since errors in dollar estimates vary in proportion of the total damage, storms are placed in categories varying from 1 to 9 as follows:

1 Less than $50
2 $50 to $500
3 $500 to $5,000
4 $5,000 to $50,000
5 $50,000 to $500,000
6 $500,000 to $5 Million
7 $5 Million to $50 Million
8 $50 Million to $500 Million
9 $500 Million to $5 Billion

*Including hurricanes

+ Additional deaths for which figures are not available.

shingles can result in later additional damage from water, so be sure to check for lost shingles after any serious wind storm.

STRUCTURAL DAMAGE

Damage to homes and other structures can result from high winds of less than tornado intensity. Careful construction will minimize this.

Homes should be secured to the foundation by bolts, or special steel anchors manufactured for the purpose. Roof construction should be secured to walls by means of special clips such as those shown in this chapter.

TORNADOES AND HURRICANES

Tornadoes

A tornado is a local storm of short duration comprised of winds moving at very high speed, usually in a counterclockwise direction. Small, severe storms forming several thousand feet above the surface during warm, humid, turbulent weather are the bearers of tornadoes—sometimes a series of two or more tornadoes accompanies a thunderstorm.

Tornadoes can occur anywhere in the United States, but no area is more favorable than the plains across North America. The greatest number of tornadoes can be expected during April, May, and

June, although they have been known to appear in December and January.

The combined action of strong rotary winds and partial action spreads destruction as the tornado passes. When a tornado sweeps over a building, the winds twist and rip at the outside at the same time that the abrupt pressure reduction in the "eye" of the tornado causes explosive pressures inside the building. Walls collapse, windows explode, and the debris alone can kill.

What Can You Do?

Weather reporting has given us the advantages of tornado watches, so that people are rarely unprepared or unwarned for an upcoming tornado. The short-term action is to stay inside, as low as possible. The long-term safety procedure, if in a tornado area, is to construct a shelter. One of the safest shelters is an underground excavation known as a storm cellar.

Location

When possible, the storm cellar should be located outside and near the residence, but not so close that toppling walls or debris can block the exit. If there is a rise in the ground, the cellar may be dug into it to take advantage of the rise for protection. The cellar should not be connected with house drains, cesspools, or sewer or gas pipes. THESE LATTER SYSTEMS ARE WHY BASEMENTS WILL NOT SUFFICE.

Size

The size of the shelter depends on the number of persons to be accommodated and the storage needs. A structure eight feet long by six feet wide, and seven feet high, will protect eight people for a short time and provide limited storage space.

Material

Reinforced concrete is the best material for a tornado shelter. Other suitable building materials include split logs, two-inch planks (treated with creosote and covered with tar paper), cinder block, hollow tile, and brick. The roof should be covered with a three-foot mound of well-pounded dirt, sloped to divert surface water. The entrance door should be of heavy construction, hinged to open inward.

Drainage

The floor should slope to a drainage outlet if the terrain permits. If not, dig a well. An outside drain is best, because it aids ventilation.

Ventilation

A vertical ventilating shaft about one foot square can extend from near the floor level up through the ceiling. This can be converted into an emergency escape hatch if the opening through the ceiling is made two feet square, and if the one-foot shaft below is easily removable. Slat gratings of heavy wood on the floor also will improve air circulation.

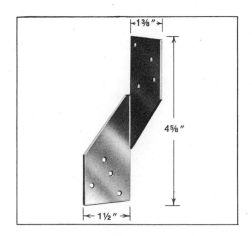

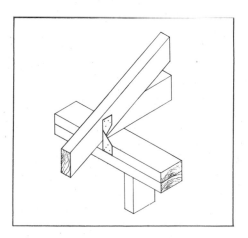

Emergency equipment

A lantern and tools—crowbar, pick, shovel, hammer, pliers, screwdriver—should be stored in the cellar to ensure escape if cellar exits are blocked by debris. Stored metal tools should be greased to prevent rusting. Your most important food item: water.

Mobile homes

These are particularly vulnerable to overturning, and should be evacuated whenever strong winds are forecast. Minimize damage by securing trailers with cables anchored in concrete footing. Trailer parks should have a community storm shelter; if not available, leave trailer park and take cover on low, protected ground.

Hurricanes

Much of the information above applies also to hurricanes, although the major danger in a hurricane is flooding. Hurricane areas are indicated in the chart provided. Your best protection during a hurricane is to stay inside, making sure outdoor objects are secured, and your windows boarded. Again, storage of drinking water is essential; next in importance are a radio and batteries. If you have time and your home is not adequately protected by boarding and high ground, move to a designated shelter.

accidents

Your home is a battlefield. Every day you must fight off the assaults of carelessly placed roller skates, traps in the form of waxed or wet floors, electric shocks, and countless other enemies.

In a recent year there were 22 million home injuries caused by accidents. More than 4.3 million were disabling injuries that resulted in bed rest for the victim. An additional 6.9 million home injuries resulted in some form of activity restriction.

Simple home accidents resulted in 26,000 deaths in one year. Falls alone accounted for nearly 10,000 of the deaths, while fire-related injuries took a toll of 5,400. Another 4,000 persons were killed by poisoning and 1,500 from accidental discharge of firearms.

There is no formula, no cure-all, for the home injury problem. All it takes to reduce the staggering home injury figures is a little caution and common sense. We will help you with a few hints, but you will have to do most of the work and planning yourself.

Alert family members to be careful of floors that have been recently washed or waxed. A simple slip can result in a serious injury. If you are repairing stairs or banisters, do not leave them unattended. A family member may lean on a railing that has not been secured and can fall down an entire flight of stairs. Bathtubs should always have grab bars and slip-resistant mats.

Cleaning agents cause burns and poisoning—and children are not the only ones injured. Label all liquids and medicines. Lock them up to keep children away. Children do not know the difference between varnish and cola drinks. Many supposed suicides are actually cases of a family member accidentally taking the wrong medicine in the middle of the night—perhaps doubling a dose of sleeping pills when he intended to take a pain medicine. A large number of additional poisonings are caused when cars are left running in a closed garage. If you are warming up your car, open the garage door. Utility gas leaks contribute to additional poisonings. If you think you smell gas, call your utility company.

Unattended pools are the scene of many drownings. A neighbor's child may wander into your yard and slip into your pool and drown. Keep swimming pools covered, or protected by a high chain link fence with a padlocked gate. Use a moisture-detection alarm which will alert you if anyone falls into your pool. Other sites of drownings are wells, bathtubs, cisterns, and other open bodies of water.

Power tools and firearms should be locked in a closet or other safe place. Putting a gun on a shelf that seems too high for Junior to reach is not always effective. Curiosity overcomes almost all barriers.

Home playground equipment contributes to

home injuries. Children fall off swings because they swing too high. Sometimes the legs of the swings are raised off the ground and tip over. Pushing, shoving, and other horseplay may result in a child getting hit by a swing. Supervise your children. Warn them of the dangers of the playground, giving them reasonable explanations for why they should refrain from certain actions.

SAFETY IN THE BATHROOM

The bathroom is such a familiar area of the house that we all tend to forget it can also be one of the most dangerous. Here, within a relatively small space, the hazards of water and electricity can combine to cause injury and even death.

Consumer activist Ralph Nader reports that nearly 900 Americans die every year as a result of injuries suffered in bathrooms, and another 187,000 are hurt seriously enough to require hospitalization or emergency room treatment. Falls, burns, cuts, electrocutions—all are possible.

The National Safety Council warns that "tile floors are a real threat when wet. Keep them wiped dry and use a non-skid mat on the floor, especially near the tub or shower where there is likely to be water on the floor."

Most fatal falls in the home admittedly involve the elderly, and for this reason special attention should be given to bathroom planning for safety for this group. But, although the elderly suffer the most severe injuries, not a single age group escapes the threat of accident.

Manufacturers are now producing bathtubs with permanent no-slip surfaces, but bathroom fixtures last for many years so that millions of homes have only the old type of tub with slippery porcelain enamel underfoot. Some type of non-skid mat or surface should be provided, along with sturdy grab bars.

Burns can occur in a bathroom probably more frequently than in any other area of a home, except around the kitchen range. The hazards of gushing hot water to infants and small children are notorious as a cause of death and disfigurement. But even adults can suffer, especially where a too-narrow shower pipe can cause a sudden rush of hot water when cold water is turned on elsewhere in the house. There are simple means to avoid this hazard. The National Safety Council recommends mixer faucets on the washbowl and a mixer valve or faucet in the shower. The most practical immediate step is simply to make sure the thermostat on the hot water heater is kept at a safe level. Water heated to 115° Fahrenheit or above is destructive to human tissue.

Electricity in combination with the water sources in a bathroom probably is the greatest hazard of all. Lighting fixtures, electrical outlets, and wall switches, all are grouped around washbowls, tubs, and showers. Family members using this room frequently have damp hands, damp bodies, or are standing on damp floors. Any malfunction in an electrical appliance can be disastrous.

The danger of shock could be completely eliminated by installation of a ground fault circuit interrupter at the fuse box of the house. These are now required in most building codes for outdoor electrical receptacles, and would be a great factor in improving home safety if they were considered equally important inside a house.

Some of the other common bathroom hazards are pinpointed in this simple home safety quiz for the bathroom provided by the National Safety Council:

Do you:
1. Have non-skid mats or textured surfaces in tubs and showers?
2. Have a sturdy grab bar for your tub or shower?
3. Have medicines clearly labeled and read the label before taking any medicine?
4. Keep medicines stored safely out of the reach of small children?
5. Dry your hands before using electrical appliances—and never operate them when you're in the bathtub.
6. Avoid using hair sprays near open flame or when smoking?

HOME ACCIDENT DEATHS BREAKDOWN, 1973

Accident Type	Death Total	Change from 1972	Death Rate
All home, all ages	26,000	-4%	12.4%
Age 0-4	3,300		
Age 5-14	1,300		
Age 15-24	2,500		
Age 25-44	3,100		
Age 45-64	4,100		
Age 65-74	3,100		
Age 75+	8,600		
Falls, all ages	9,600	-1%	4.6%
Age 0-4	250		
Age 5-14	100		
Age 15-24	50		
Age 25-44	300		
Age 45-64	1,100		
Age 65-74	1,400		
Age 75+	6,400		
Fire-related, all ages	5,400	-4%	2.6%
Age 0-4	800		
Age 5-14	500		
Age 15-24	350		
Age 25-44	750		
Age 45-64	1,300		
Age 65-74	800		
Age 75+	900		
Poisoning(solids & liquids) all ages	3,000	-14%	1.4%
Age 0-4	200		
Age 5-14	70		
Age 15-24	800		
Age 25-44	900		
Age 45-64	700		
Age 65-74	180		
Age 75+	150		
Poisoning(gases & vapors) all ages	1,000	-9%	0.5%
Age 0-4	30		
Age 5-14	40		
Age 15-24	250		
Age 25-44	250		
Age 45-64	250		
Age 65-74	100		
Age 75+	80		
Suffocation-ingested object, all ages	1,600	-11%	0.8%
Age 0-4	500		
Age 5-14	50		
Age 15-24	100		
Age 25-44	150		
Age 45-64	350		
Age 65-74	200		
Age 75+	250		
Suffocation-mechanical all ages	900	0%	0.4%
Age 0-4	500		
Age 5-14	140		
Age 25-44	60		
Age 45-64	40		
Age 65-74	30		
Age 75+	70		
Firearms, all ages	1,600	+14%	0.8%
Age 0-4	50		
Age 5-14	350		
Age 15-24	450		
Age 25-44	400		
Age 45-64	250		
Age 65-74	60		
Age 75+	40		
All other home, all ages	2,900	-3%	1.4%
Age 0-4	1,000		
Age 5-14	100		
Age 15-24	400		
Age 25-44	300		
Age 45-64	100		
Age 65-74	300		
Age 75+	700		

Source: National Safety Council Statistics

* Deaths per 100,000 population in each age group

ACCIDENT PREVENTION

INFANT'S TOYS
SHOULD BE
LARGER THAN
HIS CLOSED FIST.
SMALLER OBJECTS
WILL BLOCK
AIR PASSAGEWAY.

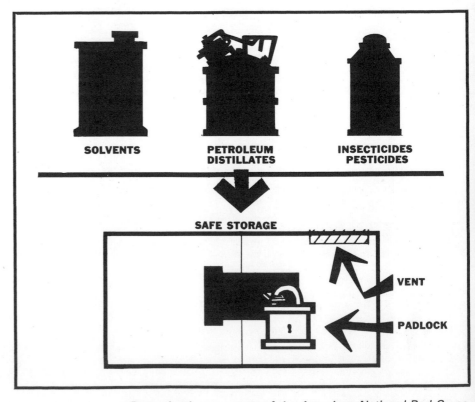

SOLVENTS   PETROLEUM DISTILLATES   INSECTICIDES PESTICIDES

SAFE STORAGE

VENT

PADLOCK

Reproduction courtesy of the American National Red Cross.

FIRST AID AT A GLANCE

AILMENT	SIGNS AND SYMPTOMS	FIRST AID
1. Poison	Symptoms vary greatly. Aids to determine whether poison was swallowed: a. Information from victim or observer. b. Presence of poison container. c. Condition of victim (sudden onset of pain or illness). d. Burns around lips. e. Breath odor. f. Pupils contracted to pinpoint size.	Check container for antidote. If none, dilute quickly and induce vomiting (except for corrosive poisons or if victim unconscious or having convulsions), maintain respiration, to preserve vital functions and seek medical assistance without delay.
2. Shock	1. Skin pale (or bluish), cold to touch and possibly moist and clammy. 2. Victim weak. 3. Rapid pulse (over 100). 4. Rate of breathing usually increases, may be shallow or deep and irregular.	Keep victim lying down. Cover him only enough to keep him from losing body heat; and obtain medical help as soon as possible.
3. Fractures and Dislocations	1. Pain and tenderness. 2. May have difficulty moving injured part. 3. Obvious deformities — swelling and discoloration.	Keep broken bone ends and adjacent joints from moving and give care for shock.
4. Burns	Skin is: 1. Red — 1st Degree 2. Blistered — 2nd Degree 3. Charred — 3rd Degree	Pain of first-degree and of a small second-degree burn can be relieved by excluding air. Three ways to exclude air from burn are: 1. Submerge in cold water for an hour or two. 2. Apply a cold pack. 3. Cover with a thick dressing or unused plastic. DO NOT use plastic to keep air off a burn on the face.
5. Heart Attack	Two principal symptoms: 1. Acute pain in chest, upper abdomen, or down left arm and shoulder. 2. Extreme shortness of breath.	Place victim in comfortable position, usually sitting up. If not breathing, give artificial respiration. Call for medical help and give prescribed medication, if any. Do not give liquids to unconscious victim.
6. Unconsciousness	Unresponsive	Keep victim warm and lying down, head turned to one side. If consciousness is not regained quickly, send for doctor. If breathing stops, give artificial respiration. Never give unconscious person food or liquids.

FIRST AID FOR CHOKING
1. Encourage victim's attempt to cough up object.
2. If object remains and victim becomes semi-conscious or unconscious, roll him to one side and strike sharp blows between the shoulder blades. (Fig. 5 front page)
3. If victim is a child, turn upside down and deliver sharp pats as above. (Fig. 6 front page)
4. Give artificial respiration if breathing stops.
5. ALWAYS seek medical help as soon as possible, even though relief is obtained.

DRUGS AND THEIR ABUSE
In cases of drug abuse emergencies, it is important that the signs and symptoms of the abuse be identified by the individual providing the immediate assistance. The type of drug, plus information on the size and age of the victim and his general condition should be provided to the drug abuse center or attending physician, if possible. For further information on drugs and their abuse, call your local drug abuse center.

Informational booklets on Drugs and Their Abuse are available at your Red Cross headquarters for 5¢ each, plus postage.

Reproduction courtesy of Golden Gate chapter of the American National Red Cross.

insurance

When all else fails you had better have insurance to cover your losses. This is not to say that insurance is a last resort. In fact, it should be the first method of protection you resort to. We have stressed that there is absolutely no foolproof method of protecting your home. If your home is an attractive target the burglar is likely to break into it and make off with your cherished possessions. The suggestions offered in this book make it less likely that you will be forced to face a burglar, but that small chance must be prepared for.

While insurance cannot replace your grandfather's watch, it can take care of the monetary loss. It can help defray the costs of rebuilding in case of fire, or buying replacement items in case of theft. Unfortunately, insurance which covers losses from crime may be hard to come by in certain high-crime areas. In fact in some high-crime areas it may be next to impossible to get insurance coverage from your local agent.

To remedy this situation, in 1970 the Federal Insurance Administrator informed the insurance commissioners of those states in which he felt there were high crime rates, that insurance must be made available through the states' FAIR (Fair Access to Insurance Requirements) Plan, or the Federal government would start writing crime insurance in those states.

California, among other states, formed its own FAIR Plan and began offering robbery-coverage, burglary, and safe-burglary coverage, or a combination of the two to provide complete protection from crime-related loss. By permitting separate purchase of robbery or burglary coverage, the program was able to offer lower premiums to its participants. To make sure policyholders are less likely to be hit by burglars, California's FAIR Plan requires an inspection prior to issuance of a policy. By making sure certain minimal security requirements are met, the Plan can offer a lower policy price.

In most participating states the Department of Housing and Urban Development (HUD) supervises the total package. HUD has been offering low-cost, noncancellable crime insurance since 1971 in states where the crime rate has soared so high that private insurers either refuse to write policies or jack up the premiums so that few people can afford to buy. The program, while considered by HUD to be a great success, is actually a failure by most standards. While it is designed to be affordable, it is still beyond the reach of many inner-city homeowners, and indeed the program has had to go begging for applicants. Another reason for the conditional failure of the program is that many private insurers are beginning to insure more

INVENTORY FORM FOR THEFT-PRONE ITEMS

for theft-prone items

Item	Year bought	Purchase price	Serial no.
Television set			
Stereo			
Radio			
Tape recorder			
Camera			
Sports equipment			
Musical instruments			
Jewelry			
Fur			
Antiques			
Stamp collection			
Coin collection			
Silverware			
Watch			
Typewriter			
Calculator			
Guns			
Bicycle			
Motorcycle			
Boat and motor			
Mower			
Power tools			
Clothing			

Keep a list of all valuables in your home. In case of burglary or fire, phone your insurance company immediately and report the incident and the serial numbers of the items.

homeowners and to give discounts for crime insurance provided the homeowner takes certain preventive measures. The major reduction in insurance premiums goes to homeowners protected by an approved burglar alarm system.

Insurance brokers in a majority of states have introduced lower cost insurance for homeowners with burglar or burglar-fire alarm systems. Reductions in premiums range from two to five percent. The highest reductions go to homeowners with central-station alarms and approved fire alarms. The lowest reductions generally go to the homeowner with a local alarm system. A reduction of about three percent may go to homeowners with a system that alerts fire or police departments directly.

In California, the minimum security requirements for the FAIR Plan include the installation of a self-locking dead latch (with trigger bolt) or a self-locking latch with deadbolt. Exterior sliding doors must have some type of deadbolt on the sill or on the edge of a fixed door. And windows must have some type of lock.

Some insurance companies are now offering discounts to homeowners who participate in some form of Operation Identification (described in the low-cost commonsense security chapter).

This book is not intended as a treatise on insurance, and could not begin to discuss the merits of various types of coverage because rates and regulations change quite often. However, if you have trouble obtaining insurance we recommend that you take advantage of your state's FAIR Plan.

And look for a policy that automatically increases the value of your home and belongings in order to protect a larger portion of the current market value of your possessions in case of loss.

PARTIAL INSURANCE

Because of high insurance premiums you may not choose to insure your home for its total value. In the case of fire insurance, for example, you may choose to insure your home for 80 percent of its value. You become a coinsurer for your house, underwriting 20 percent of the possible loss and reducing your policy cost.

The coinsurance clause found in many straight fire insurance policies encourages the homeowner to insure his home for at least 80 percent of the actual value. Therefore, if your home is worth $30,000 and you insure it for $24,000, you are covered for all losses up to that amount. If a small fire causes $12,000 worth of damage your insurance coverage pays the entire amount. But if you choose to insure your house for only $18,000, which is only three quarters of the required 80 percent coverage, the insurance company would pay only $9,000 (75 percent) of your fire loss. You would be responsible for the other $3,000 as a coinsurer.

If the value of your house is on the upswing, however, it is best to insure to 100 percent, knowing that the present 100 percent rate will lag behind market value so that you are, in essence, always a coinsurer to some extent.

home protection quiz

1. Is street lighting near your house good?
2. Is your fence higher than 40 inches? (It shouldn't be unless it is chain link.)
3. Is your yard well cared for?
4. Is your yard well illuminated?
5. Is there enough light to eliminate shadows near the sides of your house?
6. Do your trees come too close to the house, providing a staircase for the burglar?
7. Are all windows locked?
8. Are windows protected by decorative metal-work or burglar-resistant glass?
9. Do you know the difference between reachable and accessible windows? (Check Chapter Two.)
10. Do you consider a sash lock adequate protection for your windows? (Check Chapter Two.)
11. Are all windows locked when in the ventilation position?
12. Is your door frame rotting or weak in any way?
13. Do you know the best locks to use to protect a door with a rotting frame? (Check Chapter Three.)
14. Is your door rotting or weak in any way?
15. Is the gap between the door and frame smaller than 1/64th of an inch?
16. Has the hinge plate rusted through?
17. Are all doors at least 1 3/4 inches thick?
18. Have you reinforced any doors which have windows or glass panels?
19. Do you use nonretractable screws on all outside locking hardware?
20. Is your door protected from attack by a door forcer?
21. Are all hinges on the outside of the door nonremovable?
22. Do you lock the front door when you are in the back of the house?
23. Do all of your key-in-knob locks have trigger bolts?
24. If you have a mortise lock, is it protected from the cylinder puller?
25. Is your mortise lock protected from jimmying with an angling faceplate?
26. Do you have an auxiliary or secondary lock on all doors?
27. Is it true that key-in-knob locks are generally better than mortise locks? (Check Chapter Three.)
28. Do you have a high-security cylinder in your door to keep out the pickman?
29. Do you have a latch of at least half-an inch long for your mortise or key-in-knob locks?
30. Is your lock as easy to open with a pick as it is with a key?
31. Is your cylinder protected with a faceplate or cylinder ring?
32. Are primary locks better than secondary locks? (Check Chapter Three.)

33. Is your key-in-knob lock made of pressed steel?
34. Is the physical condition of door or frame a determining factor when deciding which lock to use?
35. Are all screws on padlock hasps protected?
36. Are identification codes removed from all padlocks?
37. Do you leave extra keys under door mats or in bushes? (Don't!)
38. When you lose your keys do you immediately replace your lock cylinder?
39. Are sliding doors protected with a lock as good as those on wooden doors?
40. Have you checked sliding doors to see if they can be easily removed from their track?
41. Do you have window decals alerting burglars that your house is protected by an alarm system?
42. Will your burglar alarm system accept heat sensors?
43. Is the external bell loud enough to alert neighbors?
44. Have you asked your neighbors to call the police for you in case the alarm bell sounds?
45. Are all windows or doors protected with contact switches or alarm foil?
46. Do you check your alarm periodically to see if it is functioning properly?
47. Do you walk-test your ultrasonic or microwave alarm?
48. Do you know the disadvantages of the normally open alarm circuit? (Check Chapter Four.)
49. If your alarm has a key-operated switch, is it installed above eye level to prevent picking?
50. If your alarm has an external control box, is it adequately protected by a tamper switch?
51. Is alarm wire hidden wherever possible?
52. In installing alarm foil did you prick the corners several times to ensure good contact?
53. Do your burglar and fire alarms sound different warning devices?
54. Are all appliances clean and in good repair to help reduce the possibility of an electrical fire?
55. Are easily-burned materials kept away from the stove area?
56. Are matches kept out of reach of children?
57. Are electric outlets overloaded with appliances? (They shouldn't be.)
58. Is fireplace guarded with a fine mesh screen?
59. Are ash trays made of inflammable material?
60. Are all electric heaters free of frayed wires?
61. Are all combustible materials stored in approved containers?
62. Does your family know at least two methods of escaping from the house in case of fire?
63. Do you have an early warning fire detector such as a products-of-combustion or smoke detector?
64. If you have an early warning fire detector, is it installed in a common hallway, leading to the family bedrooms?
65. Are most valuables kept in a safe deposit box?
66. Is your home safe fireproof?
67. Do you know the weak spots in your home's security?
68. Is your house ringed with perimeter lighting?
69. Is your neighborhood well lit and clean?
70. Do you have some sort of fence surrounding your property?
71. Is your front gate protected with an inexpensive burglar alarm?
72. When leaving on a vacation are interior lights connected to timers or to a photoelectric socket?
73. Do you discontinue deliveries or ask a neighbor to pick up mail and papers for you when you go out of town?
74. Do you advertise your vacation plans in the newspaper?
75. Are all unused windows nailed shut?
76. Do you have a method of locking your windows when they are in the ventilation position?
77. Are all valuables marked with some form of identification?
78. Have you and your neighbors formed a block-watchers association?
79. If you are building a new home, have you discussed security with the architect?
80. Have you limited the number of doors and windows in your new home?
81. Is your home located near the front of your lot, extending its sphere of influence onto the street?
82. Does your house design and location provide for natural surveillance of the street?
83. If you had a choice of location, would you choose to locate your home on a dead end street?
84. Have you taken advantage of such natural barriers as mountains or canyons?
85. Does your homeowners policy adequately cover you from crime-related loss?

manufacturers list

ADT Security Systems
155 Avenue of Americas,
New York, New York 10013
(Central-station alarms)

Abloy, Inc.
6212 Oakton Street
Morton Grove, Illinois 60053
(High-security locks)

Adams Rite Manufacturing Co.
4040 South Capitol Avenue
City of Industry, California 91749
(Locks for sliding doors)

Alarm Device Manufacturing Co. (ADEMCO)
165 Eileen Way
Syosset, Long Island, New York 11791
(Alarms, burglar and fire)

American La France, Inc.
4420 Sherwin Road
Willoughby, Ohio 44094
(Portable fire ladders)

Arrow Fastener Company
271 Mayhill Street
Saddle Brook, New Jersey 07663
(Stapling machines)

Arrowhead Enterprises, Inc.
Anderson Avenue
New Milford, Connecticut 06776
(Photoelectric alarms)

BRK Electronics
780 McClure Avenue
Aurora, Illinois 60504
(Early warning fire detectors)

Delta Products
P.O. Box 1147
Grand Junction, Colorado 81501
(Ultrasonic and telephone dialing alarms)

Detectron Security Systems, Inc.
Bay Street
Sag Harbor, New York 11963
(Burglar and fire alarms)

Eaton Security Products
Box 25288
Charlotte, North Carolina 28212
(Locks)

EICO
283 Malta Street
Brooklyn, New York 11207
(Home alarms)

Fichet, Inc.
Box 767C
Pasadena, California 91105
(High-security locks)

Flashguard
927 Penn Avenue
Pittsburgh, Pennsylvania 15222
(Light-activated alarms)

Functional Devices, Inc.
310 South Union Street
Russiaville, Indiana 46979
(Wireless alarms)

GC Electronics
Division of Hydrometals, Inc.
500 South Wyman Street
Rockford, Illinois 61101
(Home alarms)

Gil-Mar Enterprises, Inc.
Box 395
Miami Shores, Florida 33153
(Burglar and fire alarms)

Globe Amerada Glass Company
2001 Greenleaf Avenue
Elk Grove Village, Illinois 60007
(Burglar-resistant glass)

Ilco Corporation
35 Daniels Street
Fitchburg, Massachussets 01420
(Pushbutton locks)

J. Kaufman Iron Works, Inc.
(Windor Security Systems)
1685 Boone Ave.
Bronx, New York
(Window gates and protective grills)

Kwikset
516 East Santa Ana Street
Anaheim, California 92803
(Home alarms)

Loxem Manufacturing Company
5110 Mercantile Row
Dallas, Texas 75247
(Window and sliding door locks)

3M Security Products
3M Center
St. Paul, Minnesota 55101
(Alarms, ultrasonic and door)

M.A.G. Engineering and Manufacturing, Inc.
13711 Alma Avenue
Gardena, California 90249
(Locks and lock-changing kits)

Medeco Security Locks, Inc.
Box 1075
Salem, Virginia 24153
(Locks and cylinders)

Meilink Steel Safe Company
Box 2847
Toledo, Ohio 43606
(Home safes)

National Burglar & Fire Alarm Association
1730 Pennsylvania Ave., N.W.
Washington, D.C.
(List of recognized alarm dealers)

National Lock
Rockford, Illinois 61101
(Locks)

On-Guard Corporation of America
350 Gotham Parkway
Carlstadt, New Jersey 07072
(Home alarms)

Panel-Clip Company
24269 Indoplex Circle
P.O. Box 423
Farmington, Michigan 48024
(Clips, trusses)

Preso-Matic
3048 Industrial 33rd Street
Fort Pierce, Florida 33450
(Pushbutton locks)

Racon, Inc.
Boeing Field, International
8490 Perimeter Road, So.
Seattle, Washington 98108
(Microwave alarms)

Radio Shack
2617 West Seventh Street
Fort Worth, Texas 76107
(Alarms, burglar and fire)

Red Comet, Inc.
Box 272
Littleton, Colorado 80120
(Automatic fire extinguishers)

Sargent & Greenleaf, Inc.
1 Security Drive
Nicholasville, Kentucky 40356
(Locks)

Sargent Keso
100 Sargent Drive
New Haven, Connecticut 06509
(Locks)

Sentry
(John D. Brush & Company)
900 Linden Avenue
Rochester, New York 14625
(Home safes)

Simplex Security System
10 Front Street
Collinsville, Connecticut
(Keyless locks)

Transcience
17 Irving Avenue
Stamford, Connecticut 06902
(Wireless alarms)

Universal Security Instruments
2829 Potee Street
Baltimore, Maryland 21225
(Alarms, burglar and fire)

Westinghouse Security Systems
Westinghouse Building
Gateway Center
Pittsburgh, Pennsylvania 15222
(Central-station alarms, fire detectors)

INDEX

ALSO
in the SUCCESSFUL series

BUILD YOUR OWN HOME

As building costs soar, more and more people dream of building their own homes. Here is the book needed to make that dream a reality. From financing the project, choosing a site and subcontractors (or just friends) to the actual step-by-step construction—using the best materials and products for quality, style, and strength—the author provides a wealth of invaluable information. Basic frame construction floor plans are included for ranch, split-level, Cape Cod, and colonial styles. Fifty-two chapters in all!

Author Robert Reschke is consulting editor for *Professional Builder* magazine. BUILD YOUR OWN HOME is 320 pages, with 300 illustrations, charts, and photographs. 8-1/2" × 11". Cloth $12.00; paper $4.95 (plus 65¢ handling for single-paperback orders).

TABLE OF CONTENTS

ALSO
in the SUCCESSFUL series

BOOK OF SUCCESSFUL SWIMMING POOLS

Everything the present or would-be pool owner should know, from what kind of pool he can afford to how to get the most use and enjoyment out of it; from necessities like site selection, building permits, and finances, to accessories like lights, poolside decks, chairs, and accessory structures; from construction problems and contractors, to how to do it all by yourself. Complete sections on maintenance, repairs, and water treatment included!

Authors Ronald Derven and Carol Nichols bring a combination of skills to this book. Mr. Derven is former editor of *Home Building Business,* and Ms. Nichols is a free-lance writer with extensive experience in interior design and do-it-yourself home projects.

BOOK OF SUCCESSFUL SWIMMING POOLS is 136 pages, with over 150 photographs and diagrams. 8-1/2″ × 11″. Cloth $12.00; paper, $4.95 (plus 65¢ handling for single-paperback orders).

TABLE OF CONTENTS